D1326500

The CRICKETERS of VANITY FAIR

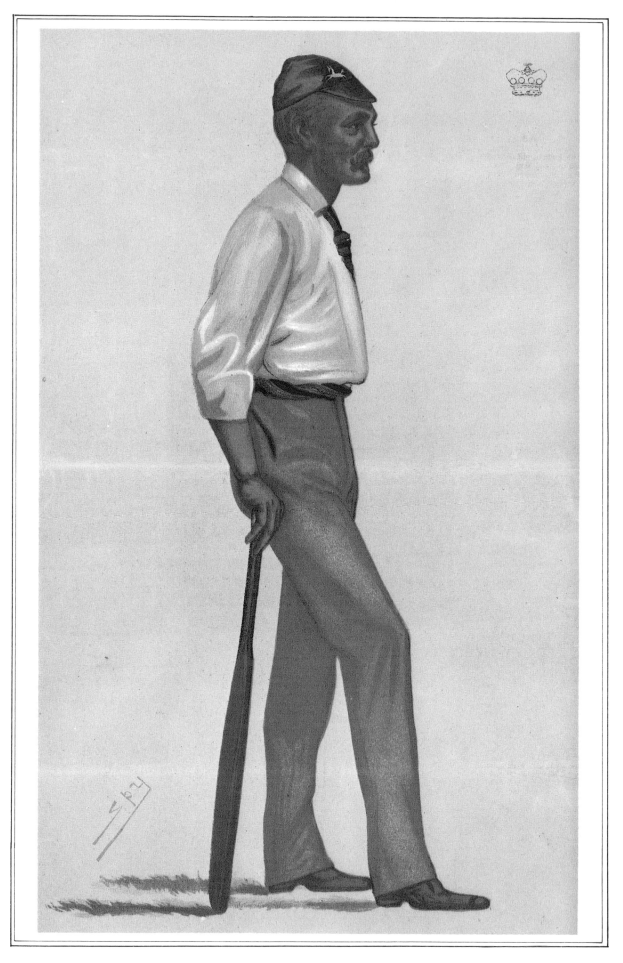

"Kent"

Lord Harris has hitherto been known from his own county of Kent to the Antipodes as a great cricketer, but he has better stuff in him than cricketers are usually made of. He is serious and earnest; he takes a great interest in public affairs, and there is good reason to expect that in due course of time he will occupy a creditable position in the House of Lords, and do service to his country. *1881 Statesmen No. 364*

The CRICKETERS of VANITY FAIR

RUSSELL MARCH

INTRODUCTION BY

JOHN ARLOTT

Grange BOOKS

Published by Grange Books
An imprint of Grange Books Limited
The Grange
Grange Yard
London SE1 3AG

ISBN 1 85627 346 6

Reprinted 1993

First published by Webb & Bower
(Publishers) Limited 1982

Printed and bound in Singapore.

Contents

The Cartoons

Introduction

JOHN ARLOTT

The *Vanity Fair* cricket prints, subject of this study by Russell March, are an important aspect of cricket pictorial art. They are, however, probably less significant in the history of the periodical in which they appeared. *Vanity Fair* began as a scandal sheet but was lifted above others of its kind by the acid skill of its early caricaturists and the trenchant criticism of its founder-editor. Having established itself as an institution it petered out in mild respectability after forty-odd years in print. At the height of its fame, which extended from the end of January 1869 until the mid eighteen-nineties, it was a considerable power in British social and political life.

It first appeared, without illustrations and sub-titled 'A Weekly Show of Political, Social & Literary Wares', on Saturday, 7 November, 1868. It made steady but unremarkable progress until the twelfth issue—that of 23 January, 1869—when it was announced that the next issue would include

A FULL-PAGE CARTOON
of an entirely novel character
PRINTED IN CHROMO-LITHOGRAPHY

and the price was sixpence.

So great was the success of the cartoon—which was of Disraeli and signed 'Singe'—that the issue was reprinted three times within four months and the price increased to a shilling. The subject of the next cartoon was Gladstone; the historic series was launched.

The third drawing, of John Bright, was by the same artist as the previous two but was signed 'Ape', the pseudonym under which Carlo Pellegrini was to become famous. The other two names for ever associated with *Vanity Fair* are Jehu Junior, the *nom de plume* under which the paper's first proprietor, Thomas Gibson Bowles, wrote the biographical notes on each week's subject, 'Man of the Day'; and Leslie Ward—'Spy'—who joined the staff in 1873 and subsequently was responsible, with Ape, for the majority of the cartoons throughout its history. Ward was to continue for some forty years, long after the other two, and to receive a knighthood.

For the first quarter century of its existence, however, the irreverent seized *Vanity Fair* as soon as it appeared on the news-stands as eagerly as they do *Private Eye* now, while the famous hastened to discover whether they were the subject of its attention. Pellegrini could be savage in his delineation of the pompous or the stupid. Above all, though, Bowles was a merciless writer in support of his original editorial undertaking to 'display the vanities of the week'.

He once wrote of a judge, 'he delights to say nasty things of, and to, solicitors; and he frightens witnesses. His voice grates and his manner repels. He has a long lip which he is able to wreathe with an unpleasant curl.' Bowles had, too, a deadly touch with his final sentences —such as, 'He can hardly remember not to forget himself',—'He has been convicted of plagiarism and decorated with the Legion of Honour',—'He has no enemies and is a sworn friend of himself.' Often he went further than that, and many libel actions were brought against him, but he fought them all, and lost only one.

A number of artists made drawings for *Vanity Fair*, among them two as eminent as W.R. Sickert and Max Beerbohm. None of them, though, commanded quite the ferocity of Pellegrini or, on the other hand, the competent, consistent, near-photographic quality of Ward's portraiture.

Bowles sold the paper in 1889; Pellegrini died in the same year; and *Vanity Fair* was never the same, nor so influential again. It slid slowly down into the early years of this century when it had become a mild 'glossy' with polite drawings and almost obsequious biographies. It was taken over, incorporated and bought out, until it perished in 1914.

The magazine's 'Men of the Day' came from many fields of activity: politics, the arts, travel, war, sport, scholarship, diplomacy, royalty. Essentially, though, it was metropolitan, with its interests, and, of course, its sales, based on London. Its material came from the Court, the law courts, parliament, the theatre, concert halls and only latterly from the city's sports grounds. It is hardly coincidence that, of Russell March's thirty-four selected cricketers, sixteen played for Middlesex, Surrey, Kent or Essex. Only one Yorkshire player—and that the patrician Lord Hawke—featured before 1902, and only two, the inescapable Hirst and Rhodes, afterwards.

To cricket collectors these plates are important. Mr March's selected thirty-four, however, are only a small proportion of *Vanity Fair*'s total output of nearly 2,500 cartoons.

Cricketers were simply not the material for the savage caricature of Pellegrini or the barbed prose of Bowles. They were folk idols, practitioners of the most popular and prestigious sport of the day. Indeed, sport was never a major concern of *Vanity Fair*. Thus, the first cricketer—W.G. Grace—did not appear until the magazine had been in publication for nine years. The only sportsmen featured before W.G. were Captain Webb, in 1875, after he had swum the Channel, and the gymnast, Captain Fred Burnaby (1876). The first jockey

—apart from cricket, horse-racing has the only double-figure sporting list—the great Fred Archer, did not appear until 1881. Grace, of course, was entitled to such prominence, not simply because he was a cricketer, but because he was a household name, an eminent Victorian whose eminence happened to stem from cricket.

The second, Spofforth, was included in 1878, on strict news value after he took ten wickets for twenty runs for the Australian touring team when, to the amazement of all England, in their first match at Lord's they beat MCC, including Grace, in a single day.

Thereafter, despite two in 1884 and three in 1892, only thirteen cricketers were featured in the thirty-one years from first publication to the end of the century. To be sure there were three in 1902 and 1903; four in 1906; but those were late days.

Beyond Russell March's select list, for the collectors whose aim is inclusion rather than exclusion, he notes other cartoons of men with unquestionable cricketing connections who appear in what *Vanity Fair*, with due objectivity, regarded as their more important capacity. Some, it must be admitted, have been claimed on the most tenuous connection with the game, including both Disraeli and Gladstone (although Gladstone's wife was a Lyttelton) with no real justification. Lord Alverstone was the senior member of the Lubbock sporting brotherhood. Several others became Presidents of MCC largely because of their standing in Debrett.

Russell March justly stresses the point that no professional cricketer was included until Bobby Abel in 1902, by which time *Vanity Fair* had long ceased to be the magazine of Bowles's original concept. That social bar alone prevents the collection being representative of the cricket of its era. Otherwise it must have included such nineteenth-century players as Shrewsbury ('Give me Arthur' said W.G. when asked which batsman stood second to himself in ability); Peel (one hundred Test wickets before 1896); George Ulyett; Pilling, by far the most accomplished wicket-keeper of the period; Briggs, Richardson, Lockwood and Lohmann. Even in Edwardian times, after the principle of including professionals had been accepted, such unquestionably outstanding players as Lilley, Barnes, Braund and J.T. Hearne were passed over, while even such important amateurs as Maclaren and R.E. Foster were never chosen. In 1884 Bonnor followed Spofforth, but no other Australian was ever featured, although Giffen, Turner, Ferris, Murdoch, Noble and the charismatic Trumper all toured England in their prime and fame. On the other hand, there is virtually no justification for such as Jephson, Gillingham and C.M. Wells; and little for E.W. Dillon—though he captained Kent when they won the Championship—or Philipson, who was included at the expense of Pilling.

Nevertheless, the select list of cricketers contains many of the great of the time, while the full, inclusive, file is interesting.

It would not be fair to describe the *Vanity Fair* cartoons as great art. Yet, apart from the delicate lithographs of the 1840s by Corbett Anderson, Basébé and Felix, it is doubtful if cricket, or any other English sport, has a more felicitous pictorial file of performers. The *Vanity Fair* drawings were skilfully executed by capable draughtsmen, and the colour-litho prints were technically extremely well made. They are colourful and pleasing as decoration, and, as they have been increasingly appreciated and collected, the full file has become an understandably valued possession.

Happily for the collector, the magazine had such a wide circulation that it should be quite possible to build a full set at no exorbitant cost. Russell March earns our gratitude by providing both a guide to the core of the matter and a full check list.

The Cricketers
of
VANITY FAIR

CHAPTER 1
The Magazine

Vanity Fair appeared on a weekly basis between November 1868 and January 1914, during which time it was probably the most successful and most discussed magazine of the age. For more than forty-five years it published comment by distinguished journalists on society, politics, fashion and other matters of the day. This mixture appealed to Victorian and Edwardian high society and to contemporary New York society, which still, apparently, looked to Europe for a lead. An advertisement of the 1890s announced that *'Vanity Fair* may be obtained in New York at the Harvard and Yale Stores, 1149 Broadway (Near Daly's Theatre), where also a large stock of *Vanity Fair* cartoons is kept.'

This influential international magazine was essentially the brain-child of Thomas Gibson Bowles, who, despite the immense handicap in Victorian times of being born out of wedlock, was able to penetrate society as no other journalist of his time. Bowles's father, Thomas Milner Gibson, became President of the Board of Trade and it was no doubt under his patronage that the boy reluctantly started work at Somerset House as a low-grade clerk.

Very soon Thomas Bowles embarked on a life-style that was inappropriate to the salary he earned, to his station in life and to his available time. Attention to his duties took second place to a stamina-sapping round of sport, parties, visits to the theatre and general high living. Bowles had great charm with women and was a welcome guest at events organized by stage and society ladies. With financial commitments far in excess of his income, he made good the deficit in two ways; by appealing to his father and through his own journalistic endeavours. By the time he reached his mid-twenties, Bowles was a regular contributor to the *Morning Post* on a wide range of subjects. He was also writing for *London Society*, the *Owl* and the *Glow Worm*. Each of these papers reflected in some measure the political and social scene of the time. There is no doubt that Bowles was a prolific and first-class journalist. In 1866, after eight years in the Civil Service, tired of his lack of progress, he resigned in order to concentrate his talents where they rightly belonged.

The first issue of *Vanity Fair* appeared two years later, in November, 1868. It was started on a total capital, part of it borrowed, of £200. At the outset sales were measured in hundreds of copies. Within six months the circulation reached 2,500. Originally the cost of the magazine was sixpence a copy or £1.10s.4d. per annum, by post, and copies were on sale in America, Australia, South Africa and France. During the early years, various set-backs were encountered but success was eventually assured by the additional enclosure of colour cartoons. The first cartoon was drawn by Carlo Pellegrini, under the pseudonym 'Singe', and was presented on 30 January, 1869. The subject was Benjamin Disraeli. Excessive demand necessitated immediate reprints. Great care in the colour printing was essential to the success of the cartoons. The issue dated 17 January, 1874 for instance, carries a notice that 'Through an accident in printing one of the colours used in the cartoon of the Duke of Edinburgh, that cartoon was not all it should have been. The whole impression is therefore being reprinted; and those who, having imperfect copies already published, will return them to *Vanity Fair* office, will receive post free in return for each, one of the more perfect copies.' With certain breaks Pellegrini, who soon Anglicized his signature to 'Ape', continued to be associated with the magazine until his death in January, 1889. The issue of *Vanity Fair* dated 26 January, 1889, contained the following, anonymous verse:

IN MEMORIAM.

CARLO PELLEGRINI.

BORN 1839.   DIED JAN. 22ND, 1889.

ALAS! poor 'Ape'!
    No fitter name, I trow,
Was e'er assumed by any joking elf
    Than that thou didst bestow
In humorous detraction on thyself.
Thy pencil-antics took so quaint a shape,
    So told of native fun
Without a wish to wound or vilify,
    That e'en the mimic'd one
Could not but smile at his own travesty.
What touch of oddity could find escape
    From thy keen, ready wit
Which, with a few deft strokes, hath oft-times made
    As palpable a hit
As e'er was dealt in limning masquerade?
At first, perchance, the great-world stood agape
    To view each well-known form
Adorn our pages in a tone of jest
    That took the town by storm;
Though soon they fell to laughing, like the rest.
    But ended is thy day,
And all thy happy portrait-quips are o'er;
    Thou'rt turned to lifeless clay,
And where was kindly gaiety before
There now is but the cypress and the crape.
    Adieu, friend 'Ape'!

It was during one of Pellegrini's breaks from the magazine, in 1873, that Leslie Ward joined the staff. Under the pseudonym 'Spy', he became the most famous and prolific of all the *Vanity Fair* artists. He had once said that, if only he could get one drawing in *Vanity Fair*, he would die happy. In the event, he contributed for forty years.

By the late 1870s, *Vanity Fair*, with its flow of comment and cartoons, was influential beyond all other similar magazines. Bowles's elevated status emboldened him to request an interview with the Prince of Wales. The interview was not granted, for some recent remarks in *Vanity Fair* regarding the Royal Household had met with disapproval.

The death of Bowles's wife diminished his zeal for the kind of journalism required to sustain *Vanity Fair*. In 1889, after twenty years' endeavour, he sold the journal to Arthur H. Evans for £20,000 and devoted himself to politics and the less demanding task of guiding the fortunes of the *Lady*. After the turn of the century, the magazine became the property of Harmsworth and was put on a more commercial basis. In 1911, William Randolph Hearst, the great American publisher, acquired *Vanity Fair* and the copyright to the title. Publication ceased in January, 1914, and *Vanity Fair* was not revived until 1949, when, for several years, it appeared as a young ladies' fashion magazine. In 1972, the title was sold to the International Publishing Corporation and, after remaining dormant for some time, became incorporated with *Honey*, a teenage fashion publication.

Several reasons have been advanced for the magazine's decline. It did suffer changes of style, particularly in the twentieth century, but the most likely explanation seems to be the gradual break-up of the very society for which it catered and from which it drew its influence and information.

CHAPTER 2
The Cartoons and the Cartoonists

More than 2,000 cartoons were published during the life of *Vanity Fair*. Among a number of artists involved, easily the most widely known were Carlo Pellegrini ('Ape') and Sir Leslie Ward ('Spy'). The early work of 'Ape' established the tradition and 'Spy' made the weekly cartoon a national institution.

The two men came from widely different backgrounds, although they became socialite friends during their period of work for the magazine. Pellegrini was born in March, 1839, at Capua, in Italy, the son of a landed aristocrat. He became the toast of Neapolitan society, with his humour, his sketches and his eccentricity. Circumstances surrounding his arrival in London, in 1864, remain obscure but, according to legend, his early days in England were frugal and penniless. He became attached to Marlborough House and the Prince of Wales's set when his thumb-nail sketches and caricatures on serviettes, table cloths and bills found royal favour. He was a short man, badly proportioned, and his very long finger-nails, as drawn in his own cartoon, suggest his admitted homosexuality. Max Beerbohm was a great admirer of Pellegrini and contributed to *Vanity Fair* in the last years of publication, showing in his work the early influence of 'Ape'. David Low, the great newspaper cartoonist, is also considered to have gained inspiration from the caricatures.

There is no doubt that it was 'Ape' who caricatured the more important and aristocratic subjects during the 1880s, but gradually the steadier and industrious Ward took on the major role. Like Pellegrini, Ward drew largely from memory, based on careful study, and gained access to Parliament and country mansions in his quest for subjects. He came from an artistic background and was of the same social class as most of the people he caricatured. He relished his involvement with his subjects and, to some extent, was perhaps too kind to them. Once his popularity was assured many put themselves forward as subjects for cartoons; some to be snubbed, others accepted.

Such was the success of the cartoons that, in 1871, a bound volume was published at two guineas. It was entitled *Vanity Fair Album* and contained 'A show of Sovereigns, Statesmen, Judges and Men of the Day, with biographical and critical notes by Jehu Junior'. This *nom de plume* concealed the identity of Bowles. In 1874, an advertisement offered a 'List of portraits contained in the volumes of *Vanity Fair Album* for the years 1869, 1870, 1871, 1872 and 1873, all of which are still in print and may be had from all booksellers'.

By 1875, the cost of the bound album increased to three guineas. Also offered were 'proof copies drawn by hand (of which only 20 exist), sumptuously bound in morocco. Price 15 guineas each.' In 1896, the album was still offered at three guineas but the proof copies were reduced in price to ten guineas and there were only ten copies on offer. Every copy was numbered and signed. The price of the bound annual album was then reduced to two guineas and remained at that figure until the magazine ceased. Six years later, in 1902, the original drawings by 'Spy' and other artists in that album were offered for sale, as well as some drawings from earlier editions. From 1905, the cartoons in the annual album were headed *Vanity Fair Supplement* and were thus distinguished from the weekly issue. They are listed under the headings 'Sovereigns', 'Statesmen' or 'Men of the Day'. After 1907, the index to 'Men of the Day' is often subtitled 'Rowing', 'Jockey', 'Cricket' and so on. During the period of publication, it was also policy to sell the cartoons separately from the magazine and in sets (for example, artists & sculptors, cricketers). There is no doubt that a great many more cartoons were printed and sold than copies of *Vanity Fair*. The issue of *Vanity Fair* dated 6 May, 1908 offered for sale, as a set, ten portraits of 'Members of the New Cabinet' post free for one guinea. The sitters included H.H. Asquith, David Lloyd George and Winston Churchill. In August of the same year a set of '22 pictures of University Oarsmen' was also offered (at fifteen shillings) and included the name of W.H. Grenfell, who later became Lord Desborough and President of MCC. Although grouped with a set of rowers, Grenfell is depicted in riding habit, though the biography mentions both his cricket and rowing interests. At another time sets of jockeys were also offered to collectors.

In 1909, *Vanity Fair* published an index of the cartoons issued to that date, grouping the subjects under various headings. The catalogue offered 'A selection of ten, shilling cartoons, for nine shillings, or twenty for fifteen shillings unframed. Prices are one shilling each except those which have become comparatively scarce.' Under the heading, 'Cricketers', are to be found thirty-two names made up of twenty-eight subjects in cricket attire, as well as C.B. Fry, J.L. Baldwin, Viscount Cobham and Earl Darnley. Any of these were available in accordance with the terms quoted, except C.B. Fry, W.G. Grace and Ranjitsinhji at 2s.6d. each and W.W. Read at 10s.6d. Ranjitsinhji is also listed under the heading 'Indian Princes' as is the Maharaja of Patiala. The Earl of Darnley is shown under the 'Miscellaneous' grouping, so it is clear that, even during the lifetime of the magazine, precise identification was not always practised.

The introduction to the catalogue stated, as mentioned already, that the price of the cartoon was increased where the prints had become comparatively scarce. The reason for such scarcity might have been an inadequate print run as much as recurrent demand. Nevertheless, it is curious that W.W. Read sold at a much higher price than others offered at a Christie's sale in March, 1912, when some of the original paintings were sold; all to the same purchaser. Bonnor and Lyttelton went for £5.15s.6d., Lord Harris for six guineas, Spofforth for £6.16s.6d., Grace for twelve guineas and W.W. Read for no less than sixteen guineas. The biggest sale ever of the original drawings took place on 28 and 29 October, 1912 and was conducted by Sotheby, Wilkinson & Hodge at 13, Wellington Street, Strand, W.C. No less than 446 lots, each lot being a single cartoon, were offered and the total sum realized was £1,455.3s.6d. Among the originals sold were those of nine cricketers, Abel (£4), Viscount Cobham (£1.10s.0d.), Earl of Darnley (£4), C.B. Fry (£2.5s.0d.), Hirst (£1), F.S. Jackson (£9.5s.0d.), G.L. Jessop (£9.10s.0d.), L.C.H. Palairet (£5) and P.F. Warner (£5.10s.0d.).

The original, of the principal artist himself, Leslie Ward (Spy), sold for £3.10s.0d.! Four years later, at Puttick and Simpson, in Leicester Square, London, Viscount Cobham was sold for ten shillings and Jessop for

one pound to a purchaser recorded as 'Low', which might indicate the interest of cartoonist David Low. It certainly shows how values could fall, in time of war. By comparison, on 15 May, 1980, at Phillips, Son & Neale, Tom Hayward fetched £260. Normally, when the original colour wash was sold by the magazine, then the stone or plate was destroyed.

When the magazine finally ceased publication, a large stock of cartoons remained. These changed hands several times before eventually reaching the collection of the late Paul Victorious, an American with an immense collection of art work and prints. On his death, the cartoons then passed to a company, Vanity Fair Ltd of Cincinnati, Ohio. Several years ago, with immense industry, an attempt was made to catalogue each subject under general headings such as 'Accountants', 'Ambassadors', 'Architects', and so on. In 1978, a well-known antiquarian bookseller in England, Clive Burden, acquired the stock of cricketers. More recently, he has purchased the American company and its entire assets, including the *Vanity Fair* cartoons.

CHAPTER 3
Cricketers and Others

The task of identifying the cricketers among 2,387 cartoons published over a period of some forty-five years is immense. John Arlott was probably the first man to address himself to the task and, as can be seen in the article published in *The Cricketer* on 22 August, 1953 (Appendix II), he made no claim to the completeness of his list of forty-seven names. Indeed, in an issue of the same magazine, published on 5 September, 1953, that great enthusiast, the late J.W. Goldman, added a further twenty-two names to the list prepared by Mr Arlott.

The task of identification is complicated for several reasons. As John Arlott observed in *The Cricketer*, there is a certain lack of sustained practice over the long years of publication in regard to the dating and/or numbering of the cartoons. In my research, I have also found the indexing at the front of the annual albums to be inaccurate on occasions. But perhaps the crucial problem concerns exactly who may reasonably be called a 'cricketer'. This decision often lies with each individual collector or enthusiast. I imagine that most readers would have no difficulty at all in defining a 'cricketer' as someone who achieved his principal acclaim or prowess on the field of play. In which case, it would not be unreasonable to expect that cricketers would all be drawn in cricket attire. The problem is that this is not always so.

One of the great cricketers and all-round sportsmen, C.B. Fry, was pictured in 1894 attired in athletic kit. The cartoon was captioned, 'Oxford Athletics'. Fry was, perhaps, an exception, in that he played cricket and soccer at the highest level as well as being an athlete of outstanding achievement. Cricket careers tend to be longer than those associated with other sports; thus, Fry is often, nowadays, thought of as pre-eminently a cricketer but the biography with his cartoon reveals his many talents. He played his first Test in February, 1896, against South Africa at Port Elizabeth, nearly two years after his cartoon was published. Another cricketer not in cricketing attire is the Hon. Ivo Bligh, who captained the English tourists to Australia in 1882–3 and who was a considerable influence in the game at the time. He was not cartooned until 1904, when he was portrayed in formal morning clothes, although in his biography due reference is made to his cricket prowess and to his status as President of the MCC in 1900.

Both the list compiled by John Arlott and the additions made by J.W. Goldman are published in Appendix II. As Mr Arlott makes clear, some of the names included therein have but a marginal connection with the game.

During the lifetime of the magazine, a great number of those portrayed in the range of cartoons were persons with a background of public school and Oxbridge, who acquired an association with cricket through their education. The trend of the day was for these young men to compete in the most popular sport of the time. In the social climate that prevailed, it was possible for someone of only modest attainment to play the occasional county or university match. Sir Pelham Warner, in his book, *Lord's 1787–1945*, tells of just such a person, Sir Edward Chandos Leigh, KC:

> The story goes that Chandos Leigh almost insisted on being given a place in the Oxford XI. That, possibly, is a little unkind, but the fact remains that he was by no means an outstanding cricketer, and we can, therefore, understand why H.D.G. Leverson-Gower, his nephew, replied, 'Heavens forbid, Uncle Eddy', when Chandos said to him during the Varsity Match of 1895, 'Well played Henwy, (he had difficulty with his r's) my boy. You bat just as I did.'

Chandos Leigh was President of the MCC in 1887.

In listing the prints which appear to have a worthwhile connection with the game, I have the advantage of what has gone before. I refer to the work of John Arlott and J.W. Goldman. Although the latter's list is somewhat unconvincing by comparison with recent *Wisden*s, it is a little more credible if pursued back in time to the *Almanack*s of the 1920s. Mr Goldman does appear to be in real error, an error repeated by some antiquarian print shops, in listing the unfortunate Lord Chelmsford (caption, 'Isandula 1881'), Commander of the British Forces in the Zulu War (1879). Perhaps Mr Goldman confuses him with the 3rd Baron and 1st Viscount (F.G.N. Thesiger), who played for Winchester in 1884 and later for Oxford and Middlesex, as well as becoming President of MCC in 1922.

I refer later to what may well have been a lapse of memory on the part of Sir Leslie Ward, in connection with the earliest cricket cartoon published; but another curious inconsistency in his book, *Forty Years of Spy*, concerns the black and white reproductions of the 7th Earl of Bessborough and the Archdeacon Benjamin Harrison. The titles quoted are 'M.C.C. Cricket' for the Earl and 'Canterbury Cricket' for the cleric, whereas the copies I located are entitled 'Fred' and 'the revised edition of the Bible'. A reference to cricket in the biography relating to the Earl, (who sat in the House as Lord Ponsonby) explains that, 'he is welcome at Lord's', but any kind of written record of the Archdeacon's efforts on behalf of the game has escaped the present writer.

Another curiosity concerns the biographies and cartoons of Lord Darnley (Ivo) and Lord Harris. Mention is made in his biography of Lord Darnley's captaincy of England in 1882–3 and of his cricket career with Cambridge University and Kent. On the other hand, the writer of the caption to the Lord Harris cartoon is clearly of the opinion that politics is more important than cricket. Yet Harris is painted in cricket gear and Darnley in formal attire, although from the remarks in his book, Sir Leslie Ward clearly identifies Ivo Bligh (Darnley) as a cricketer.

Ward also wrote, 'Among the cricketers, I first caricatured F.R. Spofforth—the demon bowler—followed by W.G. Grace and C.B. Fry, whom I portrayed as a runner. John Loraine Baldwin, the veteran cricketer, I introduced into the series in his self-propelled invalid chair; he was a very fine old man and the founder of the "Zingari" and also of the Baldwin Club.' This makes it quite clear that 'Spy' regarded C.B. Fry as a cricketer. It also makes it clear that Ward thought that the drawing of Spofforth was the first one to be completed, although, perhaps quite properly, the first cartoon to be published was that of Grace. In this matter, Sir Leslie's memory might be at fault, as Spofforth first arrived in England after Grace's cartoon was published. The inclusion of J.L. Baldwin is very pleasant because the cartoon is full of character and the subject is in much the same pose as in the painting on the staircase at Lord's, which shows the old man with his co-founders of I Zingari.

The unique and honoured position that cricket and its players occupied in the Victorian public eye was in no small way due to the stature and influence of Dr W.G. Grace, 'The Champion', who steered the game out of its 'Middle Ages' into the 'Golden Age'. No cricketer since his time has, single-handed, exerted such an influence on the game and it was right and proper that in June, 1877, 'Spy' should choose Grace as the subject of the first published cartoon in *Vanity Fair* to show a cricketer in playing attire. It is, perhaps, not the most pleasant cricket cartoon to the eye but it does indicate the majesty of the man and is still the most sought-after copy.

Perhaps the cricket cartoons should essentially relate to those whose greatest claim to public distinction lay in their cricket. Most of these subjects were depicted in cricket gear and the prints are now to be found adorning the walls and staircases of pavilions and other sporting places. However, the artists do not always appear to have given too much consideration to the choice of subject, if judged by the standards of cricketing prowess. Some subjects of modest ability are included; others of greater achievement are excluded. Despite these discrepancies, the cricket cartoons collectively reveal the popularity of the game and of its players, which reached a peak immediately prior to the First World War. In particular, the subjects chosen reflect the attitude of the time, when style was of the essence. Probably, for this reason, few prominent bowlers are included.

The vagaries of indexing and description apart, it can probably now be understood, as explained earlier, that it really is up to those interested as collectors of prints or of cricketana to decide just how tenuous or substantial the connection with cricket has to be for a subject of a *Vanity Fair* cartoon to be of real interest. My own approach was to locate all the prints listed by the earlier researchers and then, by using the resources of the National Portrait Gallery, the British Library and the Guildhall Library (City of London), to examine the complete volumes of *Vanity Fair* from genesis to demise. As a result, the titles I now go on to describe will probably satisfy all but the most devoted of collectors.

The permutations among forty-five years of cartoons are endless and require some constraints. I have listed as cricketers those portrayed in cricket gear, of which there are thirty-one. I have added C.B. Fry, included J.L. Baldwin and one further delightful cartoon, that of R.A.H. Mitchell, the Eton coach, who guided the early careers of so many of the others. In addition to these thirty-four cartoons, I have added the Earl of Darnley, for reasons already stated, and Viscount Cobham, because, at the time, he was head of the greatest cricketing family—the Lytteltons. (No less than twelve Lytteltons and Lord Cobham are shown in *Wisden*s of the 1920s. By 1979, the total reached seventeen, including the 8th, 9th and 10th Viscounts.) To round matters off, I have included Patiala, because the Maharaja organized the first All-India team to this country, in 1911, and did much to further the game in the subcontinent, and 'Rhodes the 2nd' (Sir Abe Bailey), because he fostered cricket in South Africa and financed the first tour of England by his countrymen. Lastly, the principal artists, 'Spy' and 'Ape', are added for obvious reasons. This makes a total of forty subjects.

Most of those listed, with the exception of the artists, played a great part in the development and popularity of the game but anyone might expand the list in a variety of ways. For example, it might reasonably be assumed that every President of MCC had more than a passing connection with cricket. Research has shown that, during the lifetime of the magazine (1868–1913), over twenty Presidents were depicted in *Vanity Fair*. Of this total, Lord Harris and the Hon. Alfred Lyttelton (Presidents in 1881 and 1884 respectively) are already listed

among the cricketers. Other cricketers went on to become President of MCC: Lord Hawke (1914–18), Hon. F.S. Jackson (1921) and Sir Pelham Warner (President 1950 and First Life Vice-President 1961). The Duke of Beaufort (President 1877) was portrayed twice, in 1876 and 1893. Baron Alverstone (President 1903) is unique in being portrayed no less than four times. He was a very strong character, prepared to oppose in Committee even such as Lord Harris, should occasion arise.

In addition to those cartooned who were President during the lifetime of the magazine, a number of issues show persons who held the office before the magazine commenced publication. Both sets of names are included in the list published in Appendix IV. It must be said that little or no mention of cricket or MCC is made in the biographies issued with the cartoons and it is reasonable to assume that the primary purpose for the selection lay outside their association with the game. Nevertheless, those depicted show the kind of person associated with high office in the undisputed controlling body of cricket. To that extent, they reflect the tenor and pattern of the original English rural game, which was to give to the world a new kind of attitude to sport, epitomized in that well-worn distinction between that which is and that which is not 'cricket'.

CHAPTER 4

Cricket in England

Vanity Fair lasted from the second half of Victoria's reign, through Edward VII's short span and into the era of George V. In the early years, Bowles often covered his assignments, in business and pleasure, on horseback. By 1914, the motor car had begun to entice customers from the ubiquitous railways and several cartoons featured the early aviators.

The expansion and population of the British Empire was a constant theme of discussion throughout the period. The great white settlements of Australia, New Zealand and Southern Africa were taking shape, as well as a host of lesser states. The huge subcontinent of India was being administered by the British upper classes and Indian princes were absorbing English public school attitudes. At home, privilege and rank went together and *Vanity Fair* truly reflected the passing scene. The leisured classes devoted a great deal of time and attention to pleasure and there is no doubt that cricket gradually became the activity most closely associated with the accepted ideals of manly sport. The game was fostered at public schools, perfected at university and then taken to the four corners of the Earth by the diplomats, bankers, traders and military men of the time. From England, teams of tourists went forth to the overseas countries and the *Vanity Fair* cricketers played a notable part in this movement.

W.G. Grace, the first of the cricketers cartooned in *Vanity Fair*, regarded 1870 as the beginning of his manhood and the season in which he produced some of his very best form. He was already better known than any other sportsman and soon was to develop into a hero of such proportions that he became the first national sporting idol. In his great physique and dominant personality, the Victorians saw a presence which appealed to their collective beliefs. These beliefs were reflected by a passage taken from Thornbury's *Old and New London*, published at this time:

> Apropos of Lord's Cricket Ground, we may add there is nothing in which a more visible improvement has taken place than in our sports. The prize ring, and bear garden, dog fighting and rat killing, are things of the past; but our glorious boat races, at which we are the finest in the world; cricket in which we have no rivals; and athletic sports—running, jumping the hurdles—in which we have reached the highest perfection. The Duke of Wellington attributed a great deal of his success in war to the athletic exercises which Englishmen practised in peace. The steady nerve, quick eye and command of every muscle, exercised considerable power in the battle field. On the Continent these games are almost unknown, and the biggest Frenchman or Prussian is the veriest baby in the hands of an Englishman in any physical display.

Today, we would regard such an opinion as extremely chauvinistic but readers of the time no doubt accepted it at face value. Seven years after that book was published, on 9 June, 1877, the first cricket cartoon was issued in *Vanity Fair*, that of Dr William Gilbert Grace. A little more than a year later, the second cricketer to be featured was the legendary Australian, Frederick Robert Spofforth. This was a portent of many magnificent moments in the game, when the champions of the early England v. Australia Test Matches brought great drama to an already popular sport.

Perhaps the veneration in which the players and the game were held is best illustrated by the following report, taken from the weekly magazine *Cricket*, 21 August, 1884:

> It will be a source of general gratification to cricketers if the astute person who took advantage of the Hon. Alfred Lyttelton's presence behind the wicket at the Oval last week in the match between England and Australia, to obtain his coat by false representations at his residence, has placed himself within the reach of the law. At least there is some hope that the individual is now in durance vile. Edward Lloyd, described as a porter, was brought up at Clerkenwell Police Court on Monday on two charges of obtaining articles of clothing by false pretences and Inspector Peel, of 'G' Division, procured a remand, stating it was believed he would be recognized as the man who

obtained the Hon. Alfred Lyttelton's coat from his residence while the gentleman was playing against the Australian XI. Anyone so utterly dead to the patriotic feelings of any Englishman as to utilize Mr Lyttelton's absence on the cricket field on such an important occasion deserves no sympathy. Indeed, he is not likely to get any.

An allusion to this event is contained in the 'Jehu Junior' notes to the cartoon featuring Lyttelton under the heading 'English Cricket' and published in *Vanity Fair* on 20 September, 1884. Lyttelton died in 1913 and such was the esteem in which he was held that, during the university match of the same summer, the flag at Lord's was lowered to half mast in unique tribute. In the House of Commons, Prime Minister Herbert Asquith referred to him as the example of what every English father would wish a son to become.

It could be said that, up until the 1920s, it was possible to move easily between the club and first-class game. Indeed, some might maintain that it was only the advent of the Second World War which saw the end of the gifted amateur, although before that date the game was largely a professional exercise. In reality, however, the situation was that the professionals established a considerable presence during late Victorian times. At the same time, the game retained an amateur flavour. The professionals exercised themselves as bowlers and the cavaliers gathered the runs and the plaudits.

In 1883, the batting averages showed just seven professionals in the first twenty-five places, with amateurs occupying eight of the top ten places. In bowling, the situation was reversed. Only C.T. Studd and W.G. Grace featured in the first sixteen names. By 1890, the professionals occupied the first three places in the batting averages and the first four in the bowling. The fifth man was S.M.J. Woods, who bowled only 360 overs in the season. Although the professional was beginning to take over, the game was still captained and administered by the amateurs and some irrational happenings lead one to suppose that, even at international level, cricket was still a game.

A.E. Stoddart, whose career we shall follow in some detail, if only for a short period, chose to play for Middlesex rather than for England during the two Tests played against the Australians in 1890. The second Test corresponded with the Middlesex match at Bradford, whereupon Lord Hawke, the Yorkshire captain, refused to allow two professionals, Ulyett and Peel, to play in the Test. Stoddart's actions are all the more strange since accusations were made on several occasions suggesting that he was using the game to make money. Despite such speculations, Stoddart, like so many others of gifted talent and with the right connections, moved easily between cricket at all levels.

The Hampstead Club, then, as now, was one of the leading clubs and frequently fielded sides containing a number of county players and others of scarcely less ability. Stoddart and Spofforth were both among its members. A little farther out from the metropolis was a club founded in 1735, whose status and well-being was built on local interest. The Uxbridge Club, with a picturesque ground some fifteen miles west of central London, was well established, thanks largely to the influence of two outstanding patrons, an ex-Guards officer, Colonel Greville, of aristocratic lineage, and a local, wealthy timber-merchant and forester, Charles E. Stevens. The local lord of the manor, Lord Hillingdon, was president and captain of the club and his eldest son, the Hon. C.T. Mills, followed him in playing for the club around the turn of the century on many occasions. Lord Hillingdon fostered cricket at Hillingdon Court, the family mansion, and also at his private ground at Wildernesse, Sevenoaks. Colonel Greville and Charles Stevens, over a period of many years and in varying ways, saw to ground improvements, pavilion and fencing, as well as recruiting a groundsman/professional, Harry Woods. Between them, Woods and his son served the Uxbridge Club in outstanding fashion for almost forty years. Charles Stevens built a squash court at his timber mill and encouraged cricket club members to play. In his later years, he would sit in the pavilion, browsing through *Wisden* and sending telegrams to slow batsmen suggesting retirement, or offering messages of congratulations to others for good bowling or fielding.

During late Victorian and Edwardian times a number of cricketers featured in *Vanity Fair* and others of similar background visited the ground, some on many occasions. B.J.T. Bosanquet played for the Uxbridge Club; P.F. Warner came to the ground with MCC; F.R. Spofforth and A.E. Stoddart came with Hampstead; D.L.A. Jephson with Wanderers; R.H. Spooner and G.L. Jessop came with Free Foresters as well as appearing for Uxbridge itself. Among others, E.M. Dowson (Surrey) appeared regularly for Uxbridge, while R.O. Schwarz and A.E. Vogler also played a number of games for the club, drawn by their association with Bosanquet. J.W.H.T. Douglas, Hugh de Selincourt, J.T. Hearne, A.N. Hornby and A.E. Trott were also among the many personalities who played there in the 'Golden Age'.

After the outbreak of the First World War, Jack Hobbs played many games at Uxbridge and presented to Percy Woods (Harry's son) a solid silver cigarette case inscribed with his thanks for instruction in the game of squash on Charles Stevens's court. Hobbs was stationed nearby in the Royal Air Force and was advised to play games other than cricket, in order to assist his duties in the physical training branch.

It was at the Uxbridge ground that A.E. Stoddart began a busy round of games in 1891, which serves to illustrate the cricketing activity at the time. The local paper records that it was on the sunny afternoon of 3 June, 1891, that the Hampstead XI arrived to play Uxbridge. Some players came by train and were met at the station by lads who, in various carts or trolleys,

transported their gear to the ground in the expectation of a fee of twopence, to be doubled if they were asked to whiten pad and boots. Others arrived by pony and trap. Among those in the Hampstead side was Andrew Stoddart, who had already played for England and was later to lead his country in Australia. The visitors won the game and Stoddart made 21 runs, took two wickets and one catch. (A year or two later Stoddart, at Hampstead, made 68 and F.R. Spofforth 150, out of a total of 382 against Uxbridge.)

From Cricketfield Road, Uxbridge, Stoddart returned to London and to Lord's for a county match against the growing might of Yorkshire. This game took place on Thursday and Friday and he was dismissed for a duck in both innings. On the following day, Saturday, he played for Hampstead against London Scottish with a little more success, making 18 runs and taking five wickets. Back down the hill he went to Lord's on Monday and Tuesday to play for Middlesex against Notts, getting another duck and then only 8 runs in the second innings to show for his trouble.

Wednesday was free of cricket, before another match at Lord's with Lancashire. After 37 runs in the first innings, Stoddart scored 87 not out, in under one hour, in a second innings' first wicket stand of 132. Middlesex won the game largely due to Stoddart's efforts. Saturday, 13 June, saw him play for Hampstead against Granville (Lee), a very fine side of those days, having strong ties with Surrey. He made 91 runs and took one wicket.

A fixture at the Oval against Surrey followed during the next week and then Stoddart was back to Lord's for a clash with Gloucester, a side which included W.G. and his less famous brother, Dr E.M. Grace. Stoddart totalled only 40 runs in four innings but doubtless he discussed with W.G. events of which we shall soon read. The following week, playing for Hampstead against Eltham, he made 66 runs and took six wickets. Later in the week, Middlesex played Kent at Beckenham, but Stoddart's name is missing from the team sheet. He finished the month playing in the return fixture against Uxbridge, a Saturday game played at Hampstead. This was a much-changed Uxbridge side and the game was closely contested. Both XIs managed two innings. The visitors, batting first, made 127 and 60, while Hampstead replied with 77 all out and 101 for 8. Stoddart's contribution to the game from the crease was 23 and 62 runs and a wicket in each innings.

It was during the last week of the month that a leading cricket writer of the period was able to record, 'I hear on the best authority, from the Grand Old Man himself, that the team which the Earl of Sheffield is to conduct personally to Australia next summer, is pretty well settled. As far as present arrangements go, Dr W.G. Grace will have four amateurs to accompany him . . . Mr A.E. Stoddart has also promised . . .' Lest you should think that Stoddart's June record, which we have covered in detail, was somewhat sparse evidence on which to earn selection for a touring side, it must be said that in July he made the highest innings of the season in the first-class game, scoring 215 not out in a total of 372 recorded by Middlesex against Lancashire at Old Trafford. Throughout the Australian tour, which was highly successful for Stoddart, he was described as 'Dr W.G. Grace's chief henchman'.

During 1891, Stoddart batted on twenty-two occasions for Middlesex and averaged 30.15. The end of season averages for Hampstead show:

Batting	Innings	Not Out	Runs	Highest Score	Average
A.E. Stoddart	24	1	979	153	42.56
F.R. Spofforth	6	0	200	106	33.33

Bowling	Overs	Maidens	Runs	Wickets	Average
F.R. Spofforth	137.1	52	254	38	6.68
A.E. Stoddart	451	141	961	105	8.76

All this goes to show that the selection of an England team to tour Australia was almost settled by the month of June and that the pavilion gossip of the day was much less frenetic and more reliable than it often is today. No doubt the autocratic W.G. and the selection committees had little in common but it must be remembered that these were private tours and that MCC did not assume responsibility until 1903. Stoddart's activities also demonstrate that it was possible to pass between club, county and even international matches with perfect ease. In such a fashion did most of the *Vanity Fair* cricketers pursue their summers.

Stoddart played as much for his club as for Middlesex in 1891 and his record for both as a batsman is not dissimilar. He rarely bowled for Middlesex, possibly because the task fell primarily to the professionals. It does not seem that he played before the early June game at Uxbridge and little club or county cricket was played after August. There were only nine first-class counties at the time and club fixtures were much restricted by travelling problems. The period when it was possible for club cricketers to circulate among the various levels of the game extended long past the 1890s into the early twentieth century. Meanwhile, universities and public schools were producing gifted players with the time and the inclination to play the game as a way of life.

In Uxbridge, the game had a great hold on the local community. Membership of the club was not accorded automatically on payment of a subscription: it was also necessary to be a good player! Those who supported the players were a select band and election often went by invitation or strong recommendation. Admission to the pavilion was restricted to players and a few privileged members. Ladies were welcome to the ground but were invariably barred from the pavilion, possibly because of the rudimentary nature of the washing facilities.

Some years before his death, in 1901, Colonel Greville bought the freehold of the Uxbridge ground to protect club interests. Later, at the end of the First World War, his executors offered the ground to the club for a reasonable sum but this was beyond the capabilities of the members at a time when they had played no cricket for five years. Charles Stevens immediately set in motion a fund to secure the ground and to hold the place as a memorial to those who had fallen in the great conflict. Substantial contributions were received from those of means but a great number of donations came from the less affluent, all of whom wrote touching letters of appreciation and gratitude, recalling those whose deeds they had only been allowed to follow from the boundary lines. Such was the respect in which the club was held.

It is to those who contributed at that time that the modern players must be thankful, for, by their action, they secured a piece of land in the centre of the town, which, in the 1960s, the local council found irresistible as a site for a proposed civic centre and its natural adjunct, a car park. However, having established the rights of administration over recreation, the council paid fair compensation, enabling a new ground to be purchased and developed, with magnificent facilities, now being used for county as well as club cricket, tennis, bowls and squash. Exercise and recreation are now available for many more of the local populace than those early benefactors could ever have envisaged.

Reporting a match in which a number of famous cricketers played, the local paper expressed thanks to the cricketers who delayed their lunch to enable 'the working class to watch during their dinner hour'. That may sound patronizing to us but there is no doubt that the act was appreciated at the time. The 'working class' proved the point by the manner in which they responded to Charles Stevens's appeal in 1919 and helped to secure the ground for the future.

In using as illustration the Uxbridge Club and Stoddart, the player, it is possible to show how the fortunate enjoyed a select world of their own. Over a period of a few years, no less than eight of the *Vanity Fair* cricketers played on the Uxbridge ground, most of them visiting with the clubs of their allegiance. At the same time they were actively engaged in county games and several were playing for England. Many of the players had been at the same school or university and also played a lot of country house cricket, where lavish hospitality often went hand in hand with the game itself. It soon becomes clear that cricket was a very pleasant way of life and it should be remembered that what happened at the Uxbridge Club was often repeated in many parts of the country, particularly in the Home Counties. The players achieved, without effort, publicity and hero worship unparalleled by that accorded to any other sportsmen. Soccer and rugby, although popular, were in their infancy and not regarded in the same light as cricket. Only one *Vanity Fair* cartoon is devoted to soccer (Lord Kinnaird) and only two to rugby players.

Much first-class cricket was, to the participants, an

extension of the great social contests at Lord's between the premier schools and universities. Since half the *Vanity Fair* cricketers featured in these matches at some time in their careers the scene is worth recording. *The Sunday Times* of 10 July, 1898 reported the latest Eton v. Harrow match:

> Lord's of course, represents more than meets the eye. It is the rendezvous, the 'bien entendu' of the majority of those fortunate individuals who can follow the brilliant cortège of a London season, while, moreover, to be found at the Bois of the saint who subsisted on locusts and wild honey, are those people who, so to speak, have Pullman seats in the express train of life, of those who travel through the world so rapidly that they have no time for sorrowful emotions or, in fact, for any other than pleasant ones, and Lord's is the rallying point of those latter, without doubt . . . The spectators to be seen were of a most exhilarating sort; a well dressed throng. Floreat Eton jackets with the cornflower and the 'we give them away in our society' air among those wearers, a myriad of bewitching toilettes whose owners must have broken many hearts, luncheon parties on the trim lawns and the drags with portly butlers of majestic mien opening the Irroy and Giessler, and a continual passing and re-passing of visitors, who included well-known members of London society . . . Some of these boys have already started to flirt, have already started the grand air of ennui and of the blasé onlooker at the stage of life.

More than 12,000 paying spectators watched the match, despite poor weather. It was an indication of the public appetite for society cricket.

CHAPTER 5
The Australian Connection

The influence of the English public school system was much admired overseas, not least in Australia. *The Melbourne Argus*, in 1884, a year after the famous Australian victory at the Oval, published an article which stated,

> We are not aware that any special reference has been made that in the greater attention paid to public school cricket in England as compared with Australia, one of the great secrets of her success has been found.

The writer proceeded to mention the special position, with regard to cricket, of Eton and Harrow, and continued, in reference to the pupils, 'After completing their education, they are in a position to give their attention almost solely to cricket.' In a revealing comment, the writer added, 'for as a rule, in this Colony, it is some of the wealthiest who work the hardest.'

However, the first side to tour Australia, in 1861–2, was not composed of amateur players but was entirely professional, led by H.H. Stephenson and sponsored to the extent of £7,000, in justifiable expectation of profit, by Messrs Spiers & Pond. A similar side went shortly afterwards, led by George Parr and including one amateur, Dr E.M. Grace. The teams encountered a low standard of play and it was nine years before E.M.'s brother, Dr W.G. Grace, led a further party, which included another brother, G.F. Grace as well as several other amateurs. The 'Champion' used the seven-week journey as a honeymoon and received his own and his wife's expenses, as well as a handsome tour fee. He reported that he was well satisfied with the rising standards in Australia and contemporary accounts suggest that the game was fast becoming identified with Australian pride.

James Lillywhite, who had been with W.G.'s side, returned in 1876–7. The first Test Match was played during this tour, a match in which Spofforth declined to take part because his companion, the New South Wales wicket-keeper, Murdoch, was not selected. Spofforth played in the second Test, which was staged 'for the benefit of the English professionals'. He took four wickets and 15,000 people watched as England won.

Sustained by relative success against largely professional sides from England, the Australians particularly sought to play against a touring side which included in its ranks a selection of the great amateur batsmen. In response, in 1878–9, Lord Harris led to Australia a party of amateurs and just two professionals. The English batting averages for the 1878 season were headed by W.G. Grace and Ulyett and the latter joined the tourists. Lord Harris, who was about to assume a decisive role in the future of Test Matches between England and Australia, was the subject of the third *Vanity Fair* cartoon, published in 1881, two years after the events of the tour and the subsequent ructions. A.N. Hornby was with the tourists, although his cartoon was not issued until much later, in 1891.

The England XI was defeated by ten wickets at Melbourne, in January, 1879. Spofforth took thirteen wickets in the match and became the first man to take a hat trick in Test cricket. The return Test, although eagerly awaited, was cancelled because the tourists' previous match against New South Wales was brought to a halt by a pitch invasion involving the manhandling of some players including Lord Harris, following a disputed umpiring decision. The unfortunate umpire was an Australian, called Coulthard, who later played once for his country but who, at that time, was a travelling professional umpire, locally recruited on behalf of England. Hornby apprehended the 'larrikin' who struck Lord Harris and, despite the howling mob, forced the offender to the pavilion. The riot was strongly condemned by the Australian Press and the cricket authorities. Before the game was resumed, on a later day, the

English captain absolved officials and players from blame but added that it was an occurrence impossible to forget. The New South Wales Cricket Association deplored the attack but also protested that Lord Harris was not correct or accurate in a letter written in February and published in April in London. Harris's letter cast doubts on the general standard of Coulthard's umpiring even before the unfortunate event and contained remarks about the unsporting crowds. The New South Wales Cricket Association claimed that the Australians 'have maintained the manly, generous and hospitable characteristics of the British race', and went on to remark, 'So popular amongst our people is the game of cricket [that] multitudes of all ages and classes flock to a great match,' adding that, 'So far from our crowds being the bad losers he [Lord Harris] represents, the English XIs who have visited New South Wales were never made more of than when they defeated the local team.'

Lord Harris was indisputably the most influential figure in cricket and, as a result of the dispute, the proposed 1880 tour of England by Australia was put in jeopardy. Eventually, the Australians decided to make the trip, arriving after a seven-week voyage, almost unannounced and with only three county fixtures arranged. The side was not even scheduled to play in the capital, much less in a Test Match. As the early weeks of the season passed, C.W. Alcock, the Old Harrovian and Surrey secretary, persuaded Old Etonian Lord Harris to relent. He arranged for the Sussex authorities to cancel their fixtures and for his own county to make the Oval available in September, 1880, for the first Test in England.

Lord Harris captained the England side and three Grace brothers played in the team. G.F. Grace caught a hit off Bonnor which is variously reported as travelling 115 yards off the bat or so high that the batsman ran three runs while it was in orbit. The 'Champion', W.G. Grace, scored the first Test century, with 152, and the Australian captain, W.L. Murdoch, went one run better in the second innings. At the end of the first day, Lord Harris telegraphed his wife, then in Germany: 'England 8 wickets 400, self 50.' England won by five wickets and a crowd of 40,000 attended the first two days' play but the match will perhaps also be remembered because the injured Spofforth did not play. The tour brought the Australians a creditable record of five wins, four draws and two defeats. W.G. commented loftily, 'They were quite up to our best county form but still unable to cope with a picked XI.' He went on to say that if three Tests had been played, England would still have won.

Grace's overstatement was immediately disproved. In 1881–2 in Australia, England failed to win a single Test, although drawing twice in a four-match series. Then, in August, 1882, the Australians won the only Test played, the legendary Ashes match at the Oval and Spofforth took 188 wickets on the tour.

Spofforth's cartoon was published in July, 1878, at which time he was a member of D.W. Gregory's side, the first Australians to visit England. He is depicted in the uniform of that party. The week in which the cartoon was published saw the Australians beat Leicester by 8 wickets and Spofforth take 9 for 86 in the match. He acquired a reputation as the most formidable bowler of those times. After a subsequent tour, he stayed on in England, married a Derbyshire girl and played for the county before going to London to enter the family tea business. In December, 1924, at the age of seventy-one, when he was Chairman of the Star Tea Co. Ltd, he left England on a short visit to follow the Test Matches in Australia. He died in June, 1926, at Ditton Hill Lodge, Surrey, leaving two sons and two daughters.

Spofforth and Bonnor were the only Australians cartooned in *Vanity Fair* although it must be added that S.M.J. Woods played for both England and Australia.

CHAPTER 6
New Zealand

There is some evidence that New Zealanders were very conscious of English social excesses. Their attitude can be seen in the centenary book published in 1977 by the Canterbury Cricket Association of New Zealand, compiled by R.T. Brittenden. It records that,

> Cricket in Canterbury had a natural birth. The settlement in 1850 was a planned reproduction of a piece of England in a strange land 12,000 miles away. It was a church-based design, but the bat went with the bible, for if there was to be another England, there most certainly had to be cricket . . . Just six months after the arrival of the first four ships, a cricket club had been formed.

A little later, William Guise Brittain, born in Gloucester and educated in Plymouth, a father figure in Canterbury cricket, suggested that Lyttelton should be the name of Canterbury's capital, after Lord Lyttelton of Hagley. The cricket ground became Hagley Park.

Although the settlers of the time showed a natural appreciation of the game and its traditions, the early provincial government was only too aware of the kind of rigid pattern that went with much of Victorian life in England. This is unintentionally represented in the biographies which go with the *Vanity Fair* cartoons, not least those associated with cricket. In 1860, the Christchurch Cricket Club applied for a lease of the ground at Hagley Park. This was granted subject to the provision that the club change its name to Canterbury. The reason for this was that the social club called 'The Christchurch Club' was open only to 'gentlemen of the city', whereas it had been decreed by the government that any club using Hagley Park should open membership to all who wished to play.

The first match of major character played in Christchurch was against George Parr's All England XI in 1864. Although Test Matches were not played against New Zealand until 1929–30 (in New Zealand), the country benefited from a tour by Lord Hawke's XI in 1903. This team contained many high-quality English players, including several *Vanity Fair* cricketers, among whom was B.J.T. Bosanquet. Warner, who was also in the side, reports that it was on this tour that the local word 'googly' (for something weird or unexplained) was first attached to the Middlesex man's bowling, whereby an off-break was delivered with a leg-break action.

CHAPTER 7
Southern Africa

Cricket was being played in the Cape at the beginning of the nineteenth century. Its influence moved north and east with the spread of colonization and, in Victorian times, South Africa became a popular country for cricketers to visit. Test Matches were being played by 1888. The military and public school influence was more evident here than in the antipodes. Many military men played, amateur tourists proliferated and professionals soon took advantage of pleasant and lucrative engagements.

Moving north in an attempt to fulfil Rhodes's dream of a pink map from the Cape to Cairo, the British opened up the high plateau. The pioneer column reached Fort Salisbury in September, 1890, and the evidence suggests that cricket gear travelled in the wagons. We know that a match was played between those in the column recruited in Johannesburg and the 'Rest'. In his book, *A Scantling of Time—The Story of Salisbury, Rhodesia*, G.H. Tanser wrote that the first cricket match to be reported by the Press was played in September, 1891, to mark the first anniversary of Occupation Day. Matches were undoubtedly played before that date, as the contemporary account recorded, 'Cricket is not dead but has been sleeping.'

The Salisbury Cricket Club was formed in October, 1891, and some of the earlier maps show the location of the ground on the south side of Manica Road. One of the early games on that ground was between the 'Public School Boys' and 'The World'. It is recorded that the 'Old School Tie' feeling was so strong that the name of the school attended by each player was shown on the score sheet. By 1893, despite the appalling difficulties still being faced by the settlers and the threat of Matabele attack, the number of cricket teams increased from eleven to eighteen. A little later there came an invitation from Bulawayo, in the south, to send down a side to play over Christmas, 1895. Harry Taberer, an Oxford cricket blue, was appointed captain. This expedition foundered against the adventurous appeal of the Jameson Raid; three of its leading members left to join the doomed force.

Some of the most prominent of the early administrators were devoted to the game. William Milton declared that, next to his home and his work, cricket was the only thing he cared for. He received much support from Earl Grey, who was similarly affected. Many of the men brought into the country, as soldiers and civil servants, were good sportsmen. This led to the jibe that one needed to be a good cricketer to get a good job.

The first day of 'big cricket' in Rhodesia took place in 1898, just two years after the Matabele Rebellion, when Lord Hawke's side visited Bulawayo. Apart from himself, there were two other *Vanity Fair* cricketers in the party. They were P.F. Warner and J.T. Tyldesley. In the evening, a gourmet dinner was presented by the Bulawayo Club and the menu inscribed with an invitation, 'To meet the Amateur members of Lord Hawke's Cricket XI'. Tyldesley, of course, was not an amateur, nor indeed were four other members of the party. The discrimination was normal and was accepted as the correct manner for an overseas tour to be conducted.

In his excellent book, *Cricket in Many Climes*, Warner faithfully records the different hotels the parties stayed at and also makes it clear that hospitality offered by local dignitaries did not extend to the professionals. Warner found that, 'There were a fine manly lot of fellows in Bulawayo . . .' but also, 'one man, an old Rugbeian, informed me that he had not worn a collar for nearly a year.' The information was imparted during the dinner given to the tourists and doubtless impressed the party, although Warner was too conscious of his position as a guest to comment on the matter, except later and in the manner quoted!

This was the fifth private tour that Warner made in as many years. He visited the West Indies, America, Portugal, Canada, South Africa and Rhodesia. The game was taken to the farthest points of the English speaking world by him and others of like spirit. Warner's book is dedicated to Lord Hawke, 'who has done more than anyone else to develop cricket in our Colonies'. Such cricketers embodied the essentials of Victorian and Edwardian social structure. The magnetism of both players and game was immense and many were the tales told about those who travelled far to reach the distant, isolated grounds, whereon they played. Several enthusiastic cricketers from Salisbury, 300 miles to the north of Bulawayo, who had been given the chance to play against Lord Hawke's XI, trekked for seven days in an ox-drawn wagon, across swamp and swollen rivers, losing four nights' sleep, as they sought to keep their transport rolling for fear it should bury itself deep in the mud. The effort was considered worthy of the event.

CHAPTER 8
India

Records show that cricket was played in India, by the military and traders, in the early part of the eighteenth century. The game attracted the growing attention of the native population, particularly the Parsees, who, in 1886, were sufficiently organized to bring a side to England. They enjoyed the experience and returned two years later. It was this, no doubt, that prompted the interest of Lord Hawke and of G.F. Vernon of Middlesex, who led the all-amateur side to India in 1889. Three years later, Hawke led another side, which included F.S. Jackson. At the time of the second tour, Lord Harris was the Governor of Bombay and, as well as showing a humane concern for the condition of many of those around him, he took the opportunity of promoting and supporting cricket wherever possible.

Lord Hawke's tour was on the grand scale. Racing, polo, pig-sticking and shooting went hand in hand with cricket, which was usually played on alternate days to allow for the distractions and the lavish hospitality. The interest aroused in the game at this time led to the involvement of two illustrious personalities, whose wealth and skill were put to the task of guiding cricket in India. They were the Maharaja of Patiala and the Maharaja Jam Sahib of Nawanagar (Ranjitsinhji). Ranji learnt his early cricket in India from a Cambridge man, later went to that University, became one of the most handsome of stroke players and, in 1896, with the agreement of the Australians, played the first of his games for England in the Manchester Test. In 1897–8, he toured Australia under Stoddart and his success set fire to ambition among his countrymen and fellow princes. Coaches were recruited from the English professionals, and among those who capitulated to the game was the Maharaja of Patiala, who, throughout the 1890s, engaged the very best coaches in the persons of J.T. Hearne, Brockwell and Tarrant. Patiala's sides toured Northern India and he lavished hospitality on visitors. In an attempt to establish India as an international side, he promoted and financed the first All-India side to tour England, in 1911.

Although that first tour was largely unsuccessful on the field, the idea took root. A proposed tour of India was cancelled because of the political situation in the early 1930s but the Indians returned to England in 1933, when the first Test between the countries took place at Lord's. Lord Harris had died the year before but Lord Hawke and F.S. Jackson were able to reflect on their efforts in India thirty years before.

CHAPTER 9
United States

Cricket in the United States entered its own 'Golden Age' at the same time as it did in England. At that time, tourists from England were very popular as visitors to America, particularly in Philadelphia and other eastern states. In turn, America was well favoured by the tourists as a place that was fresh and receptive to cricket.

The tourists at the turn of the century were not, however, by any means the first on the scene. In 1859, an all-professional side left Liverpool to play five matches and to travel 7,000 miles around the vast country. In 1872, what is often called 'the first team to visit America', presumably because it was led by W.G. Grace and included Hornby and the Hon. G. Harris (later Lord Harris), paved the way for the later tours organized by Lord Hawke, Warner, Ranjitsinhji and Bosanquet, between 1897 and 1900. The traffic was not one way. In 1874, the Americans visited England to play baseball and cricket and, in August, played both games at Lord's.

The Australians also visited the United States. In 1878, the full Australian side played in Philadelphia after leaving England, and testified as to the interest and ability of the Americans. Tours by visitors continued into the twentieth century. In 1905 and 1907, MCC sent official touring teams. It was during one of these tours, as described later, that the important friendship between Schwarz and Hordern was established. Since those days, regrettably, cricket in America has not been of a standard to achieve international recognition.

CHAPTER 10
The Amateurs

Many tales are told of the achievements of the *Vanity Fair* cricketers. The captions to the cartoons tell only a small part of the story. Among the amateurs, one of the best known was the Australian, George Bonnor, pictured by 'Ape' in 1884, and as fine a physical specimen of a man, particularly to Victorian eyes, as it was possible to imagine. The diminutive Italian artist produced a painting which clearly demonstrated the aggressive attitude of the hard-hitting batsman from the 'new' country. It is said that Bonnor once splintered the wood in the sight screen on the United Services ground at Portsmouth, when it was struck by a six hit from his bat. Bonnor's playing record is modest, particularly for a cricketer who toured England on five occasions, but there is no doubt he was a crowd puller and exceedingly popular.

Bonnor was one of only five cricketers whose cartoons had appeared in *Vanity Fair* up to 1884. All five played in the Oval Test in that year. Spofforth and Bonnor were in the Australian side; Lord Harris, Lyttelton and W.G. played for England. W.W. Read also played for England in that Test and achieved immortal fame by going in at No. 10, when the batting had failed (181–8) in the face of a huge Australian score. Read made 117 runs and achieved his century in 113 minutes off 36 scoring strokes. His cartoon appeared sixth, in July, 1888.

Eighteen years after the Oval Test in which Read distinguished himself, G.L. Jessop enacted what many consider the finest match-winning innings ever played in international cricket, on the same ground, against Australia, when he made 104 runs in little more than 85 minutes with a display of spectacular hitting. Indeed, the England and Australian sides of that year, 1902, are regarded as among the best ever fielded and no less than seven of the home side were the subject of *Vanity Fair* cartoons. These were Jessop (1901), Jackson (1902), Ranjitsinhji (1897), Fry (1894), Tyldesley (1906), Warner (1903) and Hirst (1903).

Several of the cricketers excelled in many forms of sport. Hylton Philipson, for example, was Amateur Rackets Champion (1891) and a well-known footballer. His attitude to cricket was cavalier and spectacular and he was reputedly the most popular man of his generation at Eton. Philipson was a Scot and a JP for Peebles, where he maintained a castle residence but he practised his profession in London and played cricket for Middlesex. 'Spy' persuaded him to pose in his legal chambers. He went to Ceylon and India with G.F. Vernon's team in 1889, and to Australia with Lord Sheffield in 1891 and with A.E. Stoddart in 1894.

Another talented sportsman was A.N. Hornby, a cricketer who also played rugby at full back nine times for England. Hornby was at Harrow, where the unorthodoxy of his batting first attracted attention. He did not go to university but played for the Gentlemen and captained Lancashire for ten years, for which county his opening partnerships with Barlow became famous.

As well as pursuing a successful cricket career, A.E. Stoddart was also a fine rugby footballer, playing for England between 1885 and 1893 and for the Barbarians in 1890–1. Later in his career, when Secretary of Queen's Club, he organized a strong club side from among the members and guests. 'Stuff' completed the cartoon showing Stoddart in club colours. His life ended tragically, by his own hand, in April, 1915, as money matters clouded his judgement. The story is fully recorded in David Frith's award winning, *My Dear Victorious Stod*.

S.M.J. Woods, a double blue at Cambridge, had the very rare distinction of representing both Australia and England at cricket and was another very good rugby player. He achieved international honours with England in 1890 and also represented the Barbarians, for which club he was an original member and, later, a committee man, as indeed was Stoddart. Woods also played soccer for Old Brightonians, Sussex and Corinthians.

Dillon (1904–5) and Wells (1893–7) were also English rugby internationals and Barbarians. Dillon achieved great things for Kent. Wells was perhaps the most unathletic looking of all those caricatured but he lived until he was ninety-two and was still playing at club level in 1925. On 9 May, 1925, playing for P.F. Warner's XI against Datchet, he (3–1) and the Warwickshire captain, the Hon. F.S.G. Calthorpe (7–2), dismissed the local side for five runs, two of which were byes!

One of the mainstays of the game of cricket, as player, captain and administrator, was Lord Hawke. He directed his attention particularly to the ultimate well-being of the Yorkshire professionals in the way of contracts, winter employment and other similar matters.

The greatest of the cricket-playing Indian princes was Ranjitsinhji. Apart from his epic performances on the field, he also produced (probably in conjunction with C.B. Fry) one of cricket's classic books, the *Jubilee Book of Cricket*, a volume 'Dedicated by Her Gracious Permission, to Her Majesty, The Queen Empress'.

Captain Edward Wynyard, DSO, was a great tourist and country house cricketer, although, according to some accounts, he was somewhat opinionated, as military men of the time often were. The biographical notes, with the reference to Ranji, reputedly refer to a dispute over fruit at the dinner table. Wynyard retired from the Army in 1903 and toured widely afterwards. He became a great influence in Hampshire cricket and often played in an I Zingari cap, worn at a military angle with a strap under the chin.

Known as the 'Lobster' and drawn in an angular pose, D.L.A. Jephson was one of the last of the lob bowlers in first-class cricket. He also wrote poetry of some merit. Modestly he wrote, 'I have been applied medicinally when the fast and medium bowlers have tried their luck in vain.' As well as playing for Surrey, he was a great club cricketer with the Wanderers and Crystal Palace. In 1900 at the Oval, in company with Bobby Abel, the pair put on 364 for the first wicket. Jephson died, aged fifty-five, at Cambridge, where he had taken to coaching, after a period on the Stock Exchange.

The Hon. F.S. Jackson played in three Harrow XIs and four Cambridge sides before becoming a Yorkshire stalwart and one of the great England cricket captains. In the 1905 series against Australia, he led his side to success. During this series, no less than nine of the *Vanity Fair* cricketers represented England. They were Hayward, Tyldesley, Fry, Jackson, Spooner, Hirst, Bosanquet, Blythe and Jessop. Jackson served with the Royal Lancaster Regiment in South Africa and commanded the 2/7th West Yorkshire Regiment in the First World War. He later took to civic works, became a JP in the West Riding and a Member of Parliament.

The most elegant batsman in the age of style was recognized as being L.C.H. Palairet, even though he only played in two Test Matches (Australia 1902). Professionally a West Country land agent, he was also a keen fox-hunter and secretary to the Taunton Vale Hunt. In 1929, he became president of Somerset, for whom he played his last game in 1907.

Another great stylist was R.H. Spooner, who played in ten Tests between 1905 and 1912, yet never toured, because of business commitments. A natural games player, he also represented England in 1903 against Wales as a rugby wing three-quarter. Commissioned into the Manchester Regiment for the South African

War, he was invalided home with enteric fever. He became land agent for Lord Londesborough but joined the Lincolnshire Regiment a week after the First World War broke out and was wounded twice. Despite the effects of his wounds and hunting accidents, he was offered captaincy of the MCC party to Australia in 1920. He accepted but was forced to withdraw.

The last survivor of the *Vanity Fair* cricketers was Lord Dalmeny, who, in 1929, inherited the title Earl of Rosebery. He died in 1974 at the age of ninety-two. Dalmeny's record as a cricketer was modest but for some, now rather obscure, reason he lent his name to cricket advertising. In the 1906 *Wisden*, his name accompanies those of Ranji, Jackson, Fry and Warner in support of cricket gear suppliers. Money can scarcely have been the reason: his fortune at the time of his death exceeded £9 million, net!

Canon F.H. Gillingham was touring in the West Indies with the Hon. Lord Tennyson's XI as late as 1927. In 1939 he was appointed Chaplain to HM King George VI. Gillingham was a noted after dinner speaker. In 1927, he made the very first outside broadcast from the cricket ground at Leyton. A front foot player, he was at his best driving, as depicted in his cartoon.

Another tremendous driver of the ball was K.L. Hutchings of Kent, who played in all the Tests in Australia in 1907 and twice against the Australian tourists of 1909. Born near Tunbridge Wells, he followed the example of three older brothers by playing for Tonbridge with distinction, in his case, for the school XI for five seasons. He joined the colours immediately on the outbreak of war and was killed in action in 1916.

C.B. Fry was the complete all-round sportsman; one of the greatest in the annals of English sport. His Olympian ideas were communicated to readers of his ill-fated magazine, published in 1904, and much of his later life was devoted to youth training for sea cadets. While at Oxford, he was captain of the cricket club and the Association football club as well as president of the athletics club. In 1901, he hit six centuries in succession and he achieved ninety-three centuries in his career. He played soccer for Corinthians, Southampton and Portsmouth, gaining an international cap in 1901 as well as appearing in the Cup Final of 1902. In 1895, only accident prevented him playing rugby in the Oxford v. Cambridge match.

The archetypal carefree spirit of the 'Golden Age' was B.J.T. Bosanquet, whose use of the 'googly' was the last great innovation in the game. At Eton, his accomplishments at cricket, soccer and the wall game far outweighed any scholastic effort. Four years up at Oriel a few years after his great friend, Plum Warner, led to a cricket blue, half-blues for athletics (hammer throwing) and ice hockey, as well as captaincy of university billiards. He also led the college side at soccer, but failed to get a degree!

The googly was the most significant development in cricket since the change from round-arm bowling some sixty years earlier. The game was transformed almost overnight and, since the revolution took place in the 'Golden Age', when most of the *Vanity Fair* cricketers were portrayed, it is a story worth recording in detail. Once again, the influence of school, university, club, county and the social round became apparent. Indeed, were it not for the gaiety surrounding the game at the time, it is unlikely that the googly would ever have been brought into being.

Before moving to Uxbridge, in 1901, the Bosanquet family lived in a large house called 'Claysmoor', situated at Enfield. It was in this house, while the billiard table was being recovered, that the brothers Bernard and Nicolas used to hurl a tennis ball at one another across the slate. Bernard discovered that, if the wrist was dropped in front of the ball at the moment of release, then Nicolas was deceived as to the direction of the break. The googly was born. The brothers moved to the garden and practised assiduously. During this period, both boys were at Eton, where, as far as R.A.H. Mitchell was concerned, cricket was a classical off-side, stroke-making game. Mitchell threatened that Bernard's selection for the XI would be jeopardized if he continued to use his pull drive; so it seemed hardly likely that he, Mitchell, would be impressed with eccentric bowling! As, at the time, Bernard was opening the bowling for Eton, he retained a somewhat uncharacteristically respectful silence.

In the 1896 match against Harrow, his century was commented on by E.M. Dowson, who played four times for Harrow and who was to become a close friend of Bosanquet in later life. 'Bosanquet was a regular thorn in the flesh', said Dowson. 'His methods were uncouth, yet I do not think more than two or three balls passed his bat.' At Oxford, Bernard bowled the googly in the nets during luncheon intervals, much to general amusement, but persevered with his fast-medium bowling and hard-hitting batting on the field. By 1900, his reputation was established sufficiently for him to become the subject of a character portrait in *Isis* (Idol No. CLXX), which read,

> He persuaded the Dons at Oriel that he was a likely man for honours but, after a closer, if superficial, inspection of the work required of him, was led to the conclusion that the theatre and games were best suited to his taste. The first time we met him, he lapped neat whisky from a tumbler and perhaps this is why 'Bos' now drinks nothing but port. Of this wine he considers himself a Connoisseur. In both his visits to America he kept up his reputation with the fair sex . . . he still receives tinted notes from many admirers on the other side.

These visits were with Warner and Ranji; later, he was to take his own side.

Bosanquet certainly bowled the googly in America where it aroused great interest. He was referred to as 'the Dook, with a Parisian name'. In 1902–3, Lord Hawke's side, led by Warner, went to New Zealand and it was during the course of a match in Australia, while on the way home, that the great Victor Trumper was bowled first ball (some accounts say third ball) with a googly. Bosanquet finished the innings with six wickets. The googly had arrived. For the next three years, Bosanquet became the most dynamic and interesting character in a game studded with cricketers of exceptional ability, whose deeds captured the imagination of the Edwardian public. His languid, effortless man-about-town attitude off the field complemented his bizarre bowling, forceful batting and brilliant fielding, all of which led him and many close associates to a stamina-sapping round of social cricket. I Zingari, Free Foresters, Incogniti and Eton Ramblers were among clubs that benefited from his appearances.

There were many greybeards at Lord's who regarded the disguised off-break as unsporting. Warner describes in his book, *My Cricketing Life*, how he was taken to task for allowing such 'stuff' to be bowled: 'It was not only bad captaincy but immoral.' Warner persisted and Bosanquet responded, although he was sometimes wildly inaccurate. Wrist-spin is now seldom practised at the highest level because it enables runs to be scored too easily, or so some people contend!

R.O. Schwarz, of Silesian parentage, who played rugby for Richmond, the Barbarians and England, was living near Bosanquet and also playing for Middlesex. He was a member of the party that Bosanquet led to America in 1901. Schwarz's career was undistinguished until 'Bos', who at that time liked to conceal his secret, accepted his friendship and instructed him as 'my only pupil'. The coaching took place in the Nursery at Lord's and in the nets at Uxbridge. The next season, Sir Abe Bailey invited Schwarz to South Africa as his secretary, with a mission to foster cricket. Later, Bailey was to write that it was not until 'Schwarz came among us' that the South African game developed. Schwarz returned to England in 1904, with the first South African side, which was sponsored by Sir Abe Bailey. Bosanquet had just returned from Australia with Warner's victorious side and had proved the key figure, often reducing the best Australian batsmen to wild slogging. His confidence abounded and, in the South Africans' first match at Lord's, he struck peak form and took nine wickets for 109 runs. The lesson was not lost on Schwarz, who had neglected the art in South Africa. He practised very hard and was bowling his googly by the third match of the tour. He finished the season as the leading South African wicket-taker. Schwarz passed the secret on to Vogler, Faulkner and Pegler, who all played for their country in Australia in 1910–11. Vogler was in England in 1905 and joined Bosanquet in the occasional game of cricket with the Uxbridge club. Vogler and Schwarz proved match winners for South Africa against England in 1905–6. The side was led by Warner and included

Wynyard and Blythe. Vogler was the leading wicket-taker, with thirty-two victims.

In Australia, a dentist, Dr H.V. Hordern, watched Bosanquet with intense interest, imitated his action and, according to his own account, 'worked it all out'. While completing his studies in Philadelphia, he also played cricket. In 1907, the MCC touring side arrived with the much-travelled Schwarz as a member. A friendship developed around their mutual interest, the googly, and Hordern returned to Australia as a fully-fledged member of the club of eccentric bowlers. He played for his country against the South African tourists in 1910–11 and, a year later, was the leading wicket-taker against J.W.H.T. Douglas's English side. This side included Jack Hobbs, one of the last *Vanity Fair* cricketers portrayed, who, with his long career, forged the link between the 'Golden Age' and modern cricket. Meanwhile, Hordern paved the way for a long and impressive line of Australian wrist-spinners.

As for Bosanquet himself, in 1905, at Nottingham, on a perfect wicket, he ensured victory over the Australians by taking eight wickets for 107. At Lord's he was not called upon to bowl. At Headingley, in a side bristling with *Vanity Fair* cricketers (Hayward, Fry, Tyldesley, Jackson, Hirst and Blythe), he came on as fourth change, took only one wicket in the Test and never played for England again. The ball with which the Nottingham feat was performed was recently presented to MCC by Reginald Bosanquet, the TV personality and journalist, who is Bernard's son. It is now on exhibition in the cricket museum at Lord's. The Hon. F.S. Jackson had replaced Warner as skipper for the series and it seems possible that the disciplined Yorkshire player, lately returned from the war in South Africa, might have found difficulty in accepting an opinionated, carefree cavalier and his eccentric bowling as a principal wicket-taker. Bosanquet quickly lost interest in the googly and reverted to opening the bowling for Middlesex as a medium pacer. He played as an all-rounder, regularly until 1908 and less frequently until 1914, and returned at Warner's request for one last season in 1919. R.L. Arrowsmith, the noted cricket writer, recalls that in club cricket, in the mid-1920s he was an up-and-down bowler but still a strong hitter.

Percy Woods, the Uxbridge professional, remembered to the end of his days the methods of Bosanquet, Schwarz and Vogler. He had no doubt that Vogler was the best bowler of the three. Schwarz found great difficulty in bowling anything other than the disguised off-break, while Bosanquet's waywardness in length was sufficient to militate against his perfect ball, which was better disguised and spun more than any of the others. His tremendous hitting captured Percy's attention more than the googly.

CHAPTER 11
The Professionals

There were several among the *Vanity Fair* cricketers who did not rush through life on a Pullman train nor take part in the junketings surrounding the Eton v. Harrow Match. I refer, of course, to the professionals. Robert Abel was the first (1902) to be featured in 'Men of the Day'. Hirst, Hayward and Tyldesley were all pictured between 1903 and 1906. Blythe and Hobbs appeared in 1910 and 1912. By that time, a subtle change was taking place in the game as a number of the great amateurs retired or took a less active interest. Even at the turn of the century, the play of the professionals was to such a standard that a contemporary cartoon issued at the time of the Gentlemen v. Players match showed the Gentlemen in the form of a sheep being led to the slaughter, with the Players represented as a butcher with chopper raised on high. But the real battle these sturdy men fought was for social acceptance. In general terms, their background was much removed from the flamboyant amateurs with whom they played; that they succeeded in closing the gap is a tribute to their professionalism in all matters.

In 1904, Bosanquet wrote several articles for publication in the national Press, offering unstinted praise and admiration of Hayward and Hirst and, 'regretting that more in the game did not emulate their ability and unselfish approach to the tide of the match, where the needs of the team always came before their own ambition, making them true sportsmen and cricketers.' D.L.A. Jephson regarded George Hirst as the greatest all-round cricketer and his own friend, Tom Hayward, as the finest ever player of fast bowling.

It would seem that such friendly acceptance was not universal. Press comment regarding MCC and the arrangements made for the banquet given to Warner's returning side, arranged at the Trocadero on Friday, 22 April, 1904 (the eve of the FA Cup Final), was published as follows:

> Some of the old stagers of the M.C.C. must be experiencing unpleasant sensations. The announcement that the club will dine its victorious representatives on their return from the Antipodes has surely shocked their ultra conservative ideas vastly. Fancy a man who is not good enough to walk onto a cricket field out of the same gateway as an amateur being invited to sit at the same table and drink the same wines as the latter. Such a thing is unprecedented in the annals of the Club. One cannot help wondering whether the pro's will be permitted to enter and leave the dining-room by the same door as the other guests.

The comment was treated with contempt by more established journalists.

The following tale illustrates the tortuous path that had to be followed by the professionals. It was published in 1906 in the magazine, *Windsor*, by Sir Home Gordon, whose contribution to cricket literature is covered by Mr E.W. Swanton in his admirable book, *Follow On*. The story goes that,

> A famous amateur, whose life was devoted to cricket, whose name was in every mouth and whose picture was in every illustrated paper, had been sitting for Mr Ward. At dinner, on the evening of the same day, the manners, morals and general behaviour of professional cricketers was being discussed. 'Spy' stoutly maintained against an opponent that they were a quiet, well-behaved and courteous set of men. To top his argument he concluded, 'I was sketching . . . this morning', mentioning the name of the famous amateur. 'I can assure you that he is a most gentlemanly man.'

Writing some years later in *Wisden* (1932), Lord Hawke referred to his own times as a cricketer and said,

> In regard to discipline generally, I am a strong believer in the right kind of friendship between the captain and the professional members of a county XI. Between that and the kind of familiarity which only breeds contempt and therefore naturally weakens the playing power of an XI by undermining the absolute authority . . . and it must be absolute . . . of the captain, there is a very wide margin.

Stern words by today's standards.

It is perhaps worth considering the value of these professional cricketers, particularly set against some of the remuneration to the administrators and 'amateurs'. In 1898, Mr F.E. Lacey was elected Secretary to MCC, on the retirement of Mr Henry Perkins, who was awarded a pension of £400 per annum. Ground staff at Lord's received £2 per week at that time. In an article written in 1915 but based on pre-war conditions, H.V.L. Stanton recorded that the average capped professional received £6 for a match won or £5 otherwise. All expenses had to be met out of that fee. For the Gentlemen v. Players fixture (outside of Test Matches, possibly the most important contest in a season), professionals received a fee of £10 and, for an England v. Australia match, the fee had been raised to £20 but only after Lohmann, Gunn, Abel, Hayward and Richardson refused to play for the £10 originally offered.

In 1906, Stoddart became Secretary to Queen's Club, something of a sinecure but offering a salary of £300 per annum. Grace received several huge sums as 'testimonials' and 'appreciations' as well as 'expenses' of various kinds. In his book, *S.F. Barnes—Master Bowler*, Leslie Duckworth recorded that Barnes, who was perhaps the greatest bowler of all time, passed out of county cricket because Church C.C. offered him an engagement at £8 per week and a benefit match. In 1903,

Barnes was paid by Lancashire £5 for a home match and £6 for an away game, with the player meeting all expenses. Lord Hawke noted that Yorkshire-capped players such as Hirst were paid £15 for an away game and £11 at home, again meeting all expenses. Comparisons with the present day are difficult to gauge because of taxation and other factors but the wages, set against the average of the time, seem good. It was sufficient, in any case to attract the professionals who graced the field and, by their very integrity and character, opened up the game for those who followed.

One such professional was Colin Blythe, who had all but retired when the First World War erupted. He was due to take a post at Eton, where so many of the amateurs had learned their cricket. Hedley Verity and Blythe were two of the best left-arm slow bowlers England ever produced and both were killed in action in their respective wars. Because of an epileptic condition, Blythe need not have joined the Kent Fortress Engineers but he met his death in 1917, aged thirty-eight. As a bowler, he was supreme at his beloved Canterbury. According to some contemporaries, the low flight of his bowling made him more awkward even than Rhodes.

Another professional was Tom Hayward, who, like Sir Jack Hobbs, eleven years his junior, was Cambridgeshire born. Both Hayward and Hobbs gave long and eminent service to Surrey and England. Hayward first saw Hobbs playing cricket on Parker's Piece and, when introduced to his boyhood idol, the young Jack was tongue-tied. Hayward was like a monarch among the Surrey professionals and his opinion was law, although always given, like his advice, in a quiet manner. After W.G., Hayward was the first batsman to pass the 'century of centuries' milestone. Together with Hobbs, as Surrey openers, the pair shared a century partnership on forty occasions.

Hayward, together with Hirst and Tyldesley, decided not to tour Australia in 1907–8, because of the terms offered. This decision led to an invitation to Hobbs to make his first tour. Hayward retired in 1914, at the age of forty-four, after twenty-one years with Surrey. Hobbs went on playing long enough to pass, in 1925, Grace's record of 126 centuries and to span cricket from the Edwardian age to modern times. He retired from cricket in 1934 and was generally accepted as the master batsman, being perfectly equipped in temperament and technique for all situations. Hobbs hit 197 centuries in first-class matches and was knighted in 1953 for services to cricket. He died in 1963, the same year as Plum Warner.

Bobby Abel, another Surrey batsman, was a veteran of forty-six by the time his cartoon was issued, in 1902. He was a diminutive figure but nevertheless a prolific scorer, who on retirement ran a cricket shop at the Oval. He visited South Africa with Major Wharton's team in 1888–9 and was top of the averages (48). In 1891–2, with Lord Sheffield's side, captained by W.G., he paid a

second visit to Australia, having been there with one of the two 'England' sides in 1887–8.

George Hirst in a career of forty years' service to Yorkshire, was the first highly successful swing bowler but he was also a fine fielder and batsman. He was described by Lord Hawke as 'the greatest county cricketer of all time'. His benefit in 1904 brought him the unprecedented sum of £3,703. A testimonial, seventeen years later, added another £700. Although he was appointed coach at Eton, in 1921, he continued to play occasionally for Yorkshire until 1929. In 1949, he was one of twenty-six professionals accorded Honorary Life Membership of MCC.

J.T. Tyldesley, of Lancashire, retired in 1923, after passing 1,000 runs in a season on no less than nineteen occasions and making forty-six centuries in the process. Like Abel, he was a small man and depended on quick footwork. He played at Trent Bridge in June, 1899. This was the match in which Grace last captained England. The side also included Hayward, Hirst, Fry, Ranjitsinhji and Jackson. In the early years of the twentieth century, Tyldesley was the only professional batsman assured of selection for England. That great cricket scribe, Neville Cardus, regarded him as a 'professional cricketer gentleman'.

CHAPTER 12
Those of Great Influence

In so short a space, it is not possible to pursue in full the diverse careers of the *Vanity Fair* cricketers, nor, indeed, to write at length regarding the history of cricket throughout the period between Grace (1877) and Dillon (1913). Occasion has already been taken to sketch in some details of the cricketers' careers after the publication of their cartoons. In conclusion, it seems right to draw together those who by deed, on or off the field, exerted much influence on the game for a considerable period. Although the original choice of subject to be cartooned followed no discernible pattern, some of those depicted did indeed become the most influential figures in the world of cricket and are now looked upon as the great men who shaped the pattern of the game.

Pride of place must go to W.G. Grace, who was engaged in the first-class game from 1865 to 1908. His career spanned the progress of the game from historical remoteness to proximity with modern times. The link was continued by Sir Jack Hobbs, who enjoyed his first full season with Surrey in 1905 and continued to play until 1934, thus establishing a direct link between the 'Golden Age' and the modern game.

Grace was a noted hurdler in his youth. He is drawn as mighty and majestic, in his twenty-ninth year, but his appearance does suggest that the cricket of his time required rather less athleticism than today's game. In contrast, Hobbs is slim and compact, with a physique which suggests that he would have been well able to adapt to modern trends. Grace was in the autumn of his career as Hobbs was moving into his prime. By the outbreak of the First World War, 'The Master' had already made sixty-five of his centuries and completed two tours, to Australia and South Africa. Grace went to Australia only once in the whole of his forty-three seasons. The two men represented the might and pride of English batting for nearly seventy years: the autocratic amateur, who organized his cricket with professional efficiency, and the courteous professional, who played the game with gentlemanly sportsmanlike decorum. Grace, of course, was also a considerable bowler and his playing record shows his versatility. Hobbs bowled very little but was the finest cover point ever seen. Together, in their different ways and times, they set examples and standards for all to emulate.

Reference has already been made to the parts played on the field by Lords Hawke and Harris but it is, perhaps, true to say that they exerted even more control as administrators. Lord Harris was President of MCC in 1895 and Lord Hawke during the war years, 1914–18. Those bare facts give little idea of the influence they both wielded. Lord Harris was Treasurer of MCC between 1916 and 1932 and Trustee from 1906 to 1916. In such positions, in such an age, he exerted pressure in all matters appertaining to cricket. That the exercise of such influence was almost always wise, reflecting his sagacity and deep love of the game, cannot disguise the fact it was an authoritarian regime. He was much concerned with precedent and the laws. At one time, he infuriated the visiting Australians by publicly measuring the width of their bats, a move which was interpreted by the Press in Australia as a reproof. This was a misunderstanding of the situation. Action was necessary to bring standards into the game at all levels and Harris supported such action. At the time, the influential Hampstead club was advertising in *Cricket* their own intention to measure the bats of all opposing clubs and advising them to bring their own gauges if they wished.

Lord Harris also recognized the harm to the game represented by throwers. Several such bowlers had taken prominent places in leading county sides. Eventually, he pledged his county, Kent, not to play against sides selecting known throwers and he himself declined to play for England if a thrower was chosen. Such positive action did much to cure the problem.

In 1922, Harris was responsible for the suspension of Dover-born Walter Hammond from the Gloucester side, on the residential qualification. Earlier, Kent had failed to pursue their own interest in the young cricketer far enough to have him sign a contract. However, those close to Harris never doubted his motives: his concern was with the registration. According to Hammond, the Gloucester Committee considered disregarding the edict but thought better of it. Such was the power and influence of Lord Harris.

Harris was captain of Kent for fifteen years (1875–89) and he held an unsurpassed affection for the game. At the age of more than seventy, he was still playing useful club cricket. High on the list of his particular cricketing favourites, stood Eton and, in 1930, when in his eightieth year, he was still playing on those famous fields, where, in the previous century, he himself had had instruction from R.A.H. Mitchell. Harris also turned much of his time to public affairs in Kent. The Memorial Garden within the walls of Canterbury Cathedral recalls his unmatched service to the community, just as that other garden at Lord's reminds us of his devotion to cricket.

Lord Hawke (1932–8) followed Harris as Treasurer to MCC and captained Yorkshire (1883–1910), during which period the club won the County Championship on eight occasions. While he played a great part in advancing the cause of the professionals, many of whom in his early years were 'given to drink', he was also a firm disciplinarian, as well as a great believer in sportsmanship. He led or promoted a great number of tours abroad and no man did more to spread the game to distant parts. The prime qualities for selection for one of his tours, apart from ability, were said to be good manners and sportsmanship. Such requirements might make the task of selection a little harder in this age. Lord Hawke's various touring sides, listed below, played 154 matches and lost only thirteen in the process.

Lord Hawke's tours

1887–8	Australia
1889–90	India
1890–1	Canada and United States
1892–3	India and Ceylon
1894	Canada and United States
1895–6	South Africa
1896–7	West Indies
1898–9	South Africa
1902–3	New Zealand
1912	Argentine

In June, 1916, at the time of his wedding, the available members of the touring teams gave a dinner in his honour and presented him with an inscribed silver salver, recalling his ten tours thus: 'To Lord Hawke, the Odysseus of Cricket'. The engraved signatures included Jackson, Bosanquet, Warner, Philipson and Fry and it was recorded that the call of duty prevented Woods and others appending their names to the roll.

Hawke captained all the tours, with the exception of the Indian tour (G.F. Vernon's XI) and the New Zealand tour. Family illness forced him to withdraw from the latter at a late date and he handed over the captaincy to P.F. Warner. Warner was a great admirer of Hawke and led in the same spirit. Throughout a long and illustrious career, Warner was connected with MCC, Lord's and Middlesex and served on the committee for almost sixty years. During the Second World War, he was Secretary to MCC and did much to keep attractive cricket alive at headquarters. Many thousands of Royal Air Force air-crew cadets stationed nearby during their early weeks have particular reason to be grateful to the Warner administration, which kindly granted them free admission to the ground during playing hours and the use of the pavilion for service instructional purposes.

Warner was made President of MCC in 1950 and created Life Vice-President in 1961. The stand named after him is a constant reminder of his presence. He was almost continuously an England selector and, during the 1920s, while living at Datchet, his riverside house was often awash with famous cricketers. Indeed it was said locally that England XIs were sometimes selected there after a Sunday morning net!

In 1903–4, he was captain of the side which brought the Ashes back to England from Australia. A controversial choice, made at Warner's insistence, was Bosanquet, taken to exploit his revolutionary bowling, a factor which both captains later agreed made the difference between the two sides. Australian newspapers of the time record the complete bafflement of their leading batsmen when faced with the eccentric spinner. There was no sign of hostility. Some thirty years later, Warner was joint manager of another successful touring side, which included Jardine, Larwood and Voce, and promoted and practised another revolutionary kind of bowling, to be styled 'leg theory'. The pros and cons of the theory need not be argued here but Warner must have pondered on how much the game had changed in the space of thirty years for him to be involved in the soul-searing controversy and resentment generated in 1932, in contrast to the good-natured acceptance of the win in 1904.

Warner's knighthood for services to cricket came in 1937. It marked him as one of the select company of those who governed the destiny of the game. Readers will also recall that it was Warner who founded *The Cricketer* and edited it for many years.

The cricketers of *Vanity Fair* were as much part of the passing scene as any of the subjects of the other 2,000 or so cartoons in the magazine. Sufficient time has now elapsed for the part they played, not only on the cricket field but in the furtherance of the game in this and other countries, to be considered in a balanced manner and to be sensibly assessed. This book sets out to do just that and also to bring the collection of cartoons together with the biographies issued at the time. As Sir Leslie Ward predicted, 'The most faithful mirror and record of representative men and the spirit of their time will be found in *Vanity Fair*.'

CHAPTER 13
Price Guide for Collectors

Original prints

John Arlott in his introduction to this book concludes: 'Happily for the collector, the magazine had such a wide circulation that it should be possible to build a full set [of *Vanity Fair* cricket prints] at no exorbitant cost'. Some eight years later this comment can only be regarded as historic, market forces during the ensuing period having produced a situation where the value of such a set is in the region of £7,000. John Arlott probably had in mind a figure of £250–300, which catalogues from the period confirm, though even then distribution was sparse and few dealers had anything like a representative stock. The situation now is more acute.

The marketing of the residual stocks of the prints discovered in the USA (see Chapter 2) appears to have triggered the attention of a wider public to the colourful charm of the prints in general and the cricket subjects in particular. The extreme example concerns E.W. Dillon, the Kent captain, which was published in 1913, and is the rarest of all the cricket prints, since circulation of *Vanity Fair* was then at a low ebb. No copies of Dillon were among the stock retrieved from America, which adds impetus to the price escalation. In 1979 the Dillon print was available for £8 including delivery and an endorsement from the vendor on the invoice: 'Hope this is to your satisfaction'. In the summer of 1989 several sales of Dillon were agreed at around £1,500 and the price is to continue to rise. Much of the present value must be attributed to the scarcity factor since copies of two other, more distinguished, cricketers were not to be found among the American stockpile, Lord Harris (1881) and K.L. Hutchings (1907). Although expensive at around £300–350 and £175–200 respectively the price of these prints contrasts markedly with that for Dillon. A curious coincidence; all three were Kent players.

Prices now being obtained for pristine examples of other prints are as follows: Grace, Spofforth, Hawke and Hobbs fall into the same bracket as Harris; while Bonnor, Lyttleton, Ranjitsinhji, Hayward and Spooner fetch about £200–250. Fry and Lord Dalmeny sell for slightly less. Read, Hornby, Stoddart, Wynyard, Jackson, Bosanquet, Tyldesley, Gillingham, Wells and Patiala have been sold for prices between £125–150, with Philipson, Woods, Hirst, Jessop and Palairet at £50 or so less. Least expensive of the prints are Blythe, Jephson, Abel and Warner, available at £45–75. All the prices quoted refer to single copy sales from reputable stockists at a given time in 1989. Prices may rise or fall. It is possible but unlikely that an isolated dealer may offer a better deal, but on the other hand the collector may like to note the prices achieved at Christie's conducted MCC Bicentenary Auction in 1987 when a copy of Lord Harris fetched £500 and Lord Hawke £400 before the addition of Buyer's commission and VAT. No doubt a large gathering of cricket lovers under one roof contributed to the prices paid, demonstrating a volatile market providing supply and demand.

The accumulation of prints relating to those associated with the game is very popular and becomes a hobby, as John Arlott says: 'for the collectors whose aim is inclusion rather than exclusion'. For such persons I would add a name or two to the popular lists: 'Spy' pictured Leo Trevor (1905 Leo) sporting a straw hat with I. Zingari colours; Lord Barrington, published in 1875 and also in 1909, was in the Eton XI for three years, two of his sons played for Charterhouse, and he spent much time at Lord's in later life; Archibald Stuart-Wortley (1901 Sports and Arts) who produced the famous 'W.G. Grace at the Wicket' as well as other sporting paintings. The list is endless and discovery is for the dedicated. Prices will be less than for the cricketers, but where the person concerned also falls into another category e.g. Mr Justice Bray 'A Man of Law and Broad Acres' then the going rate for the legal prints will be asked.

Reproductions

The high cost of the original prints has led to the marketing of, in some cases, good quality reproductions. These are but a fraction of the cost of the genuine article and while never satisfying the true collector, there is no doubt that for decorative purposes they are adequate and fill a gap in the market.

Original watercolours

The price acceleration in this field is quite remarkable, and the location of the cricketers is such as to render the possession of the set an impossibility. The original of Tom Hayward, sold for £260 by Phillips in May 1980, would now find a ready buyer at many times that figure. Watercolours of most would command substantial four figure sums and many would draw a deep breath, even at the opportunity to purchase Grace or Hobbs. To proceed to the following table, some comment is offered.

At the March 1912 sale all the cricket paintings were sold to Colonel Sloane Stanley, a considerable collector of sporting art, and these, when joined to the seven similar lots sold at the October 1912 event, formed the basis of the *Vanity Fair* items in the Christie's sale of April 1952, the catalogue to which was headed;

Catalogue of the Third Portion of Sporting Pictures
Sold by Order of

Messrs Hutchinson & Co (Publishers) Ltd by
Christie Manson & Woods Ltd of
Spencer House
27 St James Place
London   Friday April 4th 1952.

Grace was sold to a private buyer for the highest sum paid on the day while Lords Harris and Hawke went to an MCC member who shortly afterwards presented them to the club. Until recently they were on display just inside the pavilion door, but are now more securely in custody. The remainder of the lots offered went to the highly respected West End dealers, Maggs & Co. Despite featuring in the October 1912 sale, Fry and Jessop were not lots in the 1952 auction. Since that date John Arlott at some time owned Spofforth and Bonner, while Lyttelton once belonged to Hal Cohen. Dealers acknowledge that several others have passed through salerooms in recent years. Where in the table the present location is described as 'not known' there is reason to believe the painting is in private hands and the owner, quite rightly, prefers to remain anonymous.

In 1986 the original watercolour of Jephson (Spy 1902) came to light in remarkable circumstances. Jephson was a Surrey player and it is perhaps fitting that a resident of one of the flats that jostle together with the Oval in Kennington should approach the club with a very battered framed picture that Peter Large, the Librarian, recognized as 'The Lobster'. He arranged its sale at Christie's and returned the proceeds to the bemused owner. Is it reasonable to suppose that other originals are stored behind heavy furniture or in the lofts of family homes?

Enough has been written to show that over a ten year period the purchase of either original paintings or the derivative prints has been an impressive investment. For those with a less deep pocket, the reproductions capture the colourful and evocative appeal of cricket in the golden age. As ever the choice lies with the consumer and whichever range is selected it is to be hoped the pleasure gained is sufficient to satisfy.

Subject	Christie's March 1912	Sotheby's Oct 1912	Christie's Apl 1952	Phillips May 1980	Phillips Nov 1985	Christie's Oct 1986	Present Location
Bonnor	£5.77		£3.15		£2750		Australia
Lyttelton	£5.77		£12.60				NK
Lord Harris	£6.30		£11.55				MCC Library
Spofforth	£5.85		£1.80		£2200		Burden Collection
Grace	£12.60		£18.90				NK
Read	£16.80		£3.15				NK
Abel		£4.00	£1.80				Burden Collection
Fry		£2.25					NK
Hirst		£1.00	£1.80				MCC Library
Jackson		£9.25	£1.80				NK
Jessop		£9.50					NK
Palairet		£5.00	£1.80				NK
Warner		£5.50	£12.60				NK
Lord Hawke			£11.55				MCC Library
Ranjitsinhji			£1.80				NK
Philipson			£1.80				Burden Collection
Hornby			£6.30				NK
Stoddart			£3.15				NK
Woods			£3.15				NK
Hayward				£260			NK
Jephson						£400	NK

Notes to the table

1 It is most unlikely that any of the items shown in a collection will ever be available on the market again.

2 Abel and Philipson were acquired from private sources for the Burden Collection and prices paid commensurate with current values.

3 Hirst was acquired by MCC during 1988. Current value paid.

4 Twenty-one originals have been listed, leaving Blythe, Bosanquet, Lord Dalmeny, Dillon, Gillingham, Hobbs, Hutchings, Spooner, Tyldesley, Wells and Woods to be discovered.

5 Christie's 1952 sale: Grace and Hornby as single lots; Harris and Hawke, Warner and Lyttelton as pairs; Stoddart, Woods, Bonnor, and Read as a lot and the remaining seven as another lot.

MR WILLIAM GILBERT GRACE

BORN at Bristol twenty-nine years ago of a family long given to the national game of Cricket, he found himself with a father and uncles reputed famous in its pursuit, and with brothers known for excellence in its practice. Devoted therefore though he was to the medical profession, he took up the game with enthusiasm, and his natural gifts of eye and hand have made him what he is—the best cricketer that ever played. Not only has he made the highest scores off his bat against the best bowling of the day, but he fields as well as he bats, and he gets as many runs in a season as most cricketers do in the course of their lives. He once achieved as many as four hundred runs without losing his innings.

Yet his proficiency in this particular game is not his only claim to renown; for he has proved himself an admirable runner, rider, and shot; and in addition to all this he has been a student of medicine, to which he henceforth intends to devote himself, reserving his play solely for his County and the Marylebone Club. He has excited some envy but more admiration; so that a national testimonial is about to be given to him, as he deserves who has proved himself so pre-eminent in the sports that still delight his countrymen.

1877
Men of the Day No. 150

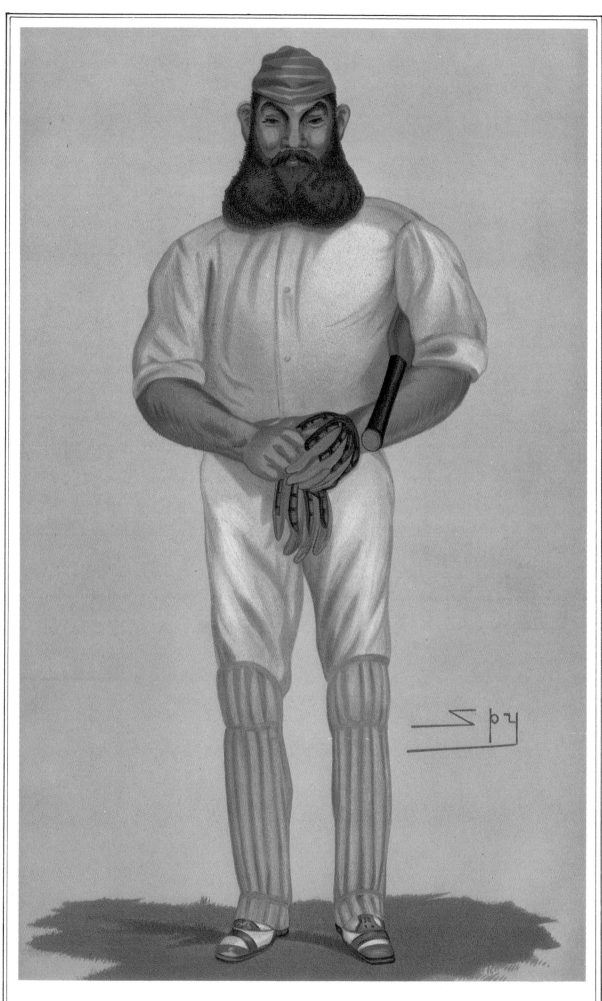

"Cricket"

MR FREDERICK ROBERT SPOFFORTH

BORN one and twenty years ago in Sydney, Mr Spofforth is Australian by origin and breeding, yet, like all the better kind of Australians, he is not distinguishable from an English gentleman. He comes, indeed, of a good English family, being the son of the late Mr Edward Spofforth, of Howden, Yorkshire, who some forty years ago distinguished himself by accompanying Captain, afterwards Sir George Grey, on an expedition to rescue the survivors of an exploring party which had adventured into the interior. He subsequently married in New Zealand the daughter of Captain McDonnell, one of the earliest settlers in that colony, established himself near Sydney, and in due course of time presented to his adopted colony the boy who has become known as "The Demon Bowler."

Mr Spofforth has been affected to the trade of banking, which he is still learning, rather than practising, in the New South Wales Bank. The love of athletic pastimes, which has been imported from Home by the Australian Colonies only to be increased and improved upon, seized him at an early age, and from his schooldays up he has been known for his quick eye, true hand, and good judgment as a bowler. He is withal of excellent manners, modest, and diffident, and has become a favourite with all who have known him in England. One of his sisters married a brother of Lady Lyttelton, whose step-sons are considered by the Australian cricketers to be the finest batsmen they have encountered since their arrival in England.

1878
Men of the Day No. 183

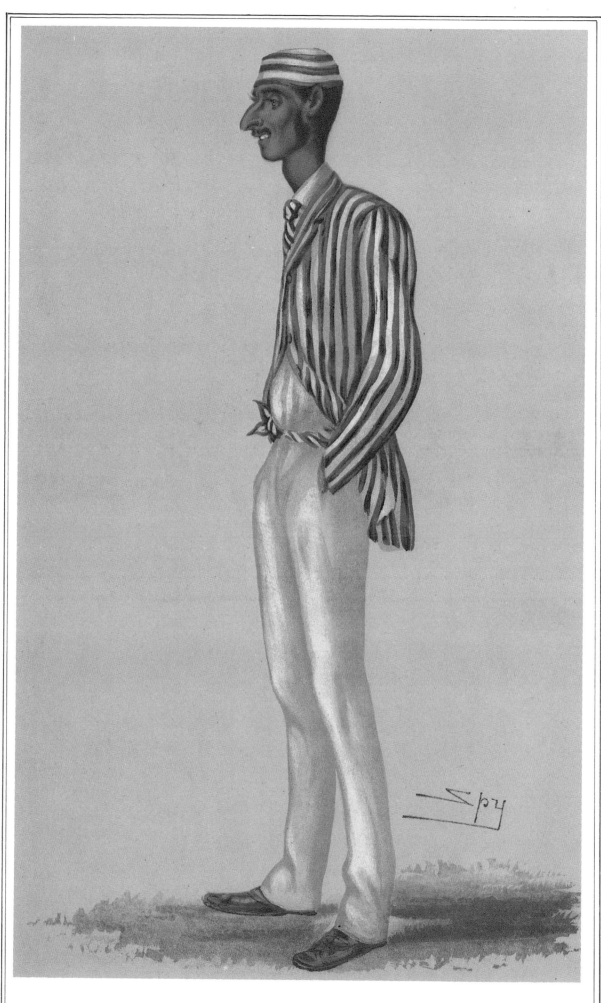

" The Demon bowler "

MR GEORGE JOHN BONNOR

HIS father was from Herefordshire, his mother was from Lancashire, and he was born eight-and-twenty years ago at Bathurst in New South Wales. He was sent to school and he went into the Bush, attached himself to sheep-farming and learnt to shoot, to ride, and to run, and has now come back to his Mother-country to represent Australian cricket as one of the Australian Eleven. He is a quiet, amiable, low-voiced, comely giant, standing six feet six in his boots, measuring forty-five inches round the chest, and weighing seventeen stone all but two pounds. He has thrown a cricket-ball 129 yards. He can bowl very fast indeed, and is a very hard hitter. He is a fine runner too, and is the hundred yards champion of New South Wales. He is neither a smoker nor a drinker, he is gentle and good-humoured, and is altogether a most excellent specimen of the Greater Briton.

1884
Men of the Day No. 313

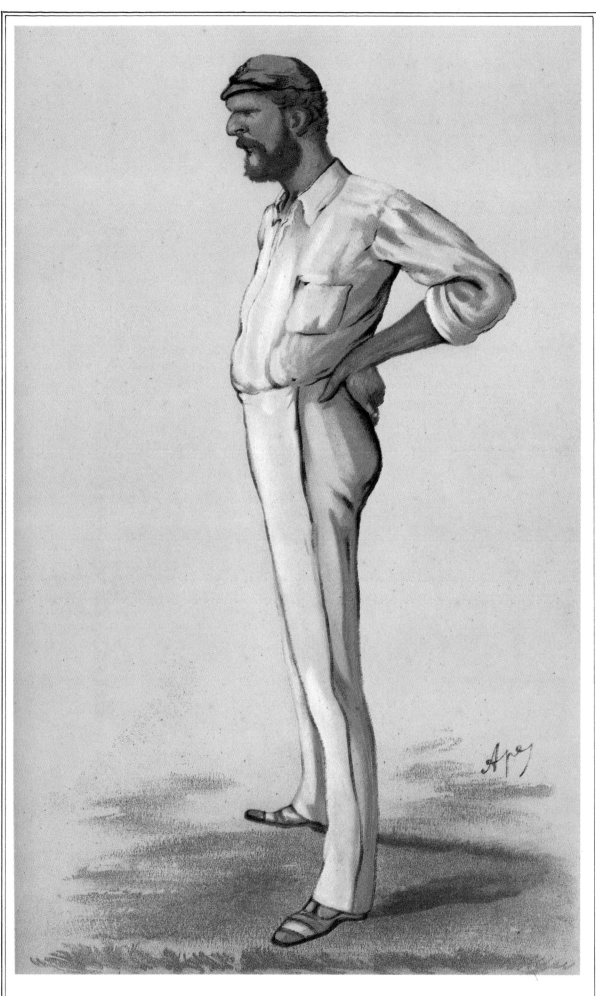

"Australian cricket"

THE HON. ALFRED LYTTELTON

MR LYTTELTON is the eighth son of the late Lord Lyttelton. He was born seven-and-twenty years ago, and is an excellent young man of good manners and of good report. By profession he is a barrister, and, as such, is second "Devil" to the present Attorney-General, who honours him with especial confidence. It is, however, as one of the lights of English Cricket that he is best known, and especially as a wicket-keeper. He is considered one of the best of the amateur players. He is very popular. He recently lost his overcoat.

1884
Men of the Day No. 314

"English cricket"

MR WALTER WILLIAM READ

HE was born at Reigate nearly thirty-three years ago; but his birth and parentage are enshrouded in middle-class obscurity. Probably no man has so many admirers who know nothing of him beyond his excellence at a certain game; but the reason that so little is known of Mr Read's early life is probably the fact that there is nothing about it worth knowing. Beyond a mild commercial education, his attainments are mostly physical, and due rather to the natural aptitude of such qualities as a "straight eye" than to any particular training in his youth. At a very early age Mr Read, like many other boys, began to play rough cricket in the fields and alleys; and he soon showed that capacity for the game upon which he has since built his reputation. By pure instinct—for he had no early tuition—he held his bat straight; and one day he was seen doing so by the Professional, Jupp, who thereupon took him under his wing, with the result that he made his *début* as one of the Surrey Eleven at the early age of seventeen years. Since then he uncertainly represented his county in the field until half-a-dozen years ago, when means were found to retain his services permanently at the Oval as Assistant Secretary to the County Club. This was good business both for Surrey and for Mr Read.

Mr Read is quite one of the best bats in the world. He plays very straight and hits all round with much freedom, so that no amateur Eleven is now complete without him. His off-drives are unequalled, and the way in which he lengthens a "long hop" on the off, sending it between point and mid-off with the speed of a round shot, is a thing to be seen and not forgotten. When he is fairly set, he is the second best run-getter we have. He is also a useful field, being considered a safe catch "in the country." He can keep wicket with the best of them, and though, in order to save his hands for batting, he does not always do so, he once kept it for Surrey while the Yorkshire Eleven scored 388 runs, without allowing them a single extra; and he sometimes bowls rather ineffective "lobs."

Mr Read's performances with the bat are known to everyone; but he can also perform in other ways. He is an Association footballer of some reputation, and he has won prizes for walking. He can also skate well; and the eye which enables him to place a cricket ball where there is no fieldsman in wait for it, also enables him to nurse billiard balls as few amateurs can nurse them. He is very popular with the Proletariat, which speaks of him familiarly as "Walter," though he is more widely known as "W. W." He is, or has been, a master in a select academy. He is also said to be something in the City.

1888
Men of the Day No. 406

"W. W."

MR HYLTON PHILIPSON

OF his early history little is known beyond the fact that he was born at Tynemouth three-and-twenty years ago; but during those years he has developed a certain straightness of eye which has now made him famous amongst University men. After four years of schooling "at Hawtrey's" he was sent to Eton, where, as a dry-bob, he learnt more about racquets, tennis, football, and cricket than he did of any of those other, and still drier, subjects for which the cost of an Eton education is supposed to be incurred by more or less deluded parents or guardians; so that by the end of his sixth year he was Captain of the Eton Field Game, and, having twice done battle for Eton at Lord's, had come to be recognised among his schoolfellows as a good match-playing bat and a fair wicket-keeper who might always be relied upon. Four years ago he went up to New College, and, although his University career has been seriously impeded by doctors, who led him to suppose that he had a heart, he has since become as well known in Oxford as he was at Eton. He has beaten Cambridge in the Single Racquet Match by four games to love; he has acquired his "Blue" as an Association footballer; he has represented Oxford as a tennis player; and, after being twice included in the Oxford Eleven without being beaten by Cambridge, he is now about to end his Oxford career as Captain of the Eleven, which is the proudest position to which a University cricketer can attain.

Mr Philipson is not a great batsman and he cannot bowl; but he does well behind the sticks in a position in which it is a great advantage for a captain to be. Notwithstanding the successive defeats which his Eleven have suffered during the season, he is full of hope as to the event of the big match which begins at Lord's on Monday, and he means to check the tide of success which has been flowing so strongly in favour of Cambridge all the year.

When he is not in flannels he wears a high collar round his neck, and looks proportionately uncomfortable in consequence.

1889
Men of the Day No. 429

Oxford Cricket

MR ALBERT NEILSON HORNBY

FOUR-AND-FORTY years ago he was born to a Blackburn mill-owner, who was so full of the sporting instinct that he added to his reputation as a keen rider to hounds that of Parliamentary representative of the people of Blackburn. At Harrow he quickly attracted attention by his sublime indifference to the educational advantages of the place and by the startling unorthodoxy of his batting; and though he failed to achieve great reputation as a scholar, he was put into the School Eleven so soon as he was as high as his bat; so that he presently appeared at Lord's as the smallest cricketer there known, and the little idol of his schoolfellows, who put him on a high pedestal and worshipped him and his extraordinary agility under the style of "Monkey"; by which name he is still known. Having learned as little as he well could at Harrow, they naturally tried to make a business man of him; but, being unable to expel Nature, they failed. For he constantly forgot to occupy the office stool, being led astray by his exceeding love of cricket; thus inciting in his father much wrath, which was only tempered by paternal satisfaction when he ran up a big score. And so he was chosen to play for the Gentlemen; since which time he has shown his style wherever cricket is played, from England to Australia; has headed the Gentlemen's batting averages, and has captained the County of Lancashire very admirably for ten years. He was so good a bat that he was constantly the first man put up against "stone wall" Barlow; he is a perfect field; and he is one of the best and most appreciative captains that have ever led an eleven to victory. He has also made his mark in the Rugby football field, and being one of the best backs that England has produced, he speedily earned his international colours, playing with great judgment and showing his opponents all the value of a timely "punt" on a wet day. He is among the best riders to hounds in Cheshire, of whom he is quite the boldest; and he has two little boys who ride two little ponies with their father and all their father's dash. He is a brilliant but uncertain shot; and he is very handy with a terrible pair of fists.

He is imbued with all the virtues that make an Englishman dear to his fellows. But he is no orator; and it is told of him how, having been asked by his fellows to represent them in Parliament, and having devoted three days to the careful preparation of his first speech, he rose with less complacency than that with which he has faced an enraged mob of larrikin thirsters for his blood to lamely explain that he had "decided not to stand." Yet it is quite certain that he could, if he would, storm any Radical constituency in Southern Lancashire. He is a cheery, kind-hearted fellow, whose consideration for the Lancashire Professionals is a byword; and his popularity is quite extraordinary. He married into a literary family, but he does not take his views from books: of which he is supposed to have succeeded in reading "Handley Cross" alone. He goes to bed early; he hates a tall hat; and he always plays cricket with an uncovered head.

He is gifted with much courage; and he is always ready to stand by a friend. He lives at Nantwich, where he has a cricket-ground of his own.

1891
Men of the Day No. 513

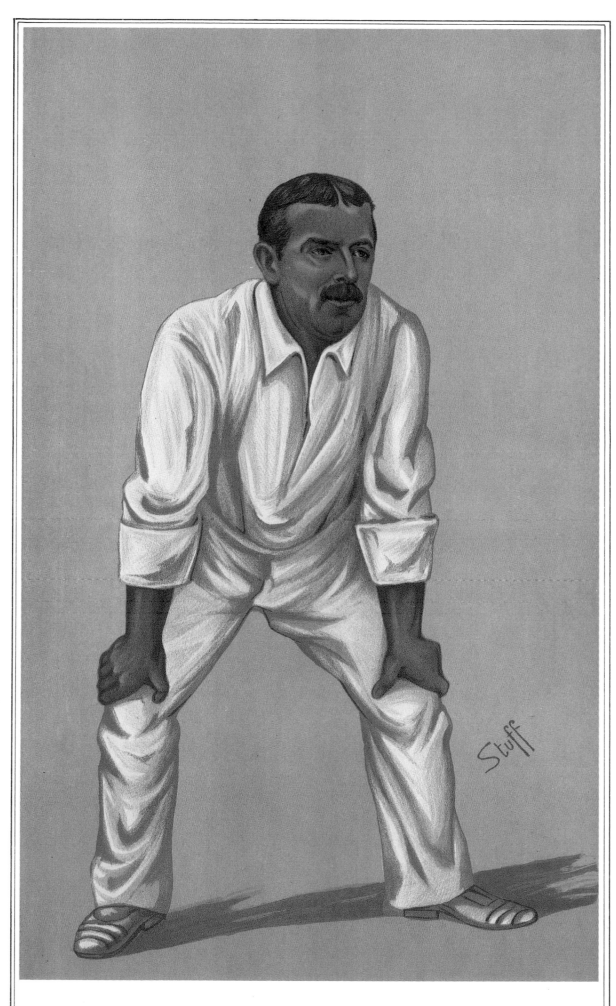

"Monkey"

MR ANDREW ERNEST STODDART

H IS birthday was the wedding-day of the Prince of Wales, and he is consequently nine-and-twenty years of age. Although his father was a colliery-owner in Durham and lived so far North as South Shields, the boy very soon tended towards St John's Wood, where he took his first lessons in cricket at a private school. He joined the Hampstead Club, and as he grew older began to hit harder, till, seven years ago, Mr A.J. Webbe saw greatness in him, and took him "on tour." He made a century-and-a-half in the big Jubilee match between the Gentlemen of England and the M.C.C.; he became the record scorer, making 456 for the Stoics; he won the Trophy with the English cricketers in New Zealand four years ago; and he has been twice in Australia as an English cricketer. His batting is strong and free, and as brilliant as stylish; in the field he covers more ground than any rival; and he is quite a useful change bowler: so that he is the best all-round gentleman cricketer of his years that we have.

He is more. Nine years ago—two years before he rose to the rank of a county cricketer—he began to play football for his county; and he has been the best three-quarter back of his generation and Captain of the Rugby Union International team. He is so keen upon the game that he has been known to save himself for a big match by staying in bed until it was time to take the field; yet it is believed that he will now, after an unusually long career of excellence as a footballer, and after twice having suffered concussion of the brain, give up playing the ball with his foot in favour of cutting it with his bat or with his racquet. For he is a first-rate player of racquets and of tennis; he can run; and he can jump hurdles.

He is a great favourite at Lord's, where the ground-men love him and speak of him admiringly as "Stod." He has pleasant manners and a soft voice, with which he can sing patter songs well to his own accompaniment. He is always so neatly dressed that he is known to a section of the cricketing public as "The Masher"; yet, being a modest fellow, he is quite without "side."

He is a very quiet, fine young fellow with very many friends and no enemies.

1892
Men of the Day No. 543

"A big hitter"

MR SAMUEL MOSES JAMES WOODS

HE is an example of Colonial greatness, for he was born of colonists at Glenfield, near Sydney, four-and-twenty years ago. But he soon thought of crossing the seas (or his parents did for him); for he first learned to play football and cricket at Brighton College (where also he may have learned some other things); so that that comparatively humble abode of learning has been honoured by the educational production of a deadly wicket-taker. He went to Cambridge and took wickets with such execution that by last year he had been made Captain of the University Eleven. And when he could not play cricket he played Rugby football; so that before he left Cambridge he was known as a player of the summer game for the Gentlemen, and of the winter game as one of the English Fifteen. But, like most Australians, he is a better cricketer than he is a footballer, for in the kicking game he is not quite so good a man as he looks, being a brilliant "loafing" player indeed, but inclined to avoid unnecessary entrance into the scrummage.

He became really famous at Kennington Oval in June of last year, when Surrey was yet an unbeaten county. Playing for Cambridge, he made runs and stayed a "rot" which seemed to have set in amongst his fellows; then bowled with such fury and yet so accurately, that he established a "funk" even amongst such experienced batsmen as those in whom Surrey put her trust for runs; so that Cambridge, after being in a minority on the first innings, beat Surrey and scored a little triumph for the University and a great one for Mr Samuel Moses James Woods. He has made a First-Class County of Somerset, and he is now looked upon as one of the finest cricketers that either England or Australia has yet produced; for his fast right-hand bowling is very deadly with its quick break back; he has much judgment; he is a reliable bat and a safe catch; and he plays his best when he is fighting an uphill game. Moreover, he has never yet been known to tire either in the toughest of matches or on the hottest of days.

He has put off the Colonial, having taken so kindly to English ways that he is now engaged in learning to make beer in a Somersetshire brewery. He is a good-tempered, bullet-headed young fellow, with a fine physique and a finer constitution. He is known as "Sammy," and it is said that he can speak his mind.

1892
Men of the Day No. 544

"Sammy"

LORD HAWKE

NEARLY a century-and-a-half ago one Edward Hawke, Rear-Admiral of the White, achieved so splendid a victory over the French that he presently got command of an expedition fitted out to act against the French coast; and having hoisted his flag aboard the *Royal George*, he led his fleet in pursuit of the enemy, whom he signally defeated off Bellisle, thereby making himself very memorable in our naval annals, and still more so in those of the French. He was the worthy beginning of the Barony to which Martin Bladen Hawke, seventh Baron, succeeded nearly five years ago. He was born two-and-thirty years ago, and in due course went to Eton, where he began to justify himself of his motto—(which is "Strike")—better and more wholesomely than ever did labour-monger; hitting up runs at cricket with increasing vigour. He went on to Magdalene College, Cambridge, and continued to hit them up. He is now Captain of the 3rd Battalion of the Princess of Wales's Own Yorkshire Regiment, as well as Captain of the Yorkshire County Cricket Eleven; for which he has done great things, being the only amateur player who has regularly captained the County Eleven; and this he has done for ten years. And though, owing to an injury to his hand, he did not accomplish much for his county last year, he yet most creditably managed a team in America in the autumn; sparing no trouble to make his own men comfortable nor to teach the Americans cricket. And he is now about to take another team to India; for he is always full of keen love for the game, and though not so sure a run-getter as are some of his fellows, yet his zeal for, and his knowledge of, it make him an excellent and popular captain.

He is a member of the Carlton and of the Bachelors', and a good-looking, pleasant, modest fellow; and though he is not as yet a great statesman he is a good Conservative.

He is a light-hearted bachelor.

1892
Statesmen No. 601

"Yorkshire Cricket"

MR CHARLES BURGESS FRY

HE is scion of an old Sussex family, and it will be two-and-twenty years on Wednesday next since he was born at Croydon; but it is not yet three years since, becoming Senior Scholar of his year at Wadham College, he took up to Oxford the reputation of the best athlete at Repton (where he was taught sport enough by Mr Forman to become Captain of the Cricket Eleven and of the football team) and grew into the famous Dark Blue hero that he now is. In that short space he has achieved much, winning a triple Blue and long jumping beyond the British record in his first year; repeating his triumphs, propelling his twelve stone over a space of 23 ft. 6½ in. (the world's record), and running a dead heat for the Inter-'Varsity Hundred Yards in his second; and holding out still further promise (in spite of a bruised heel) in his third. He has compassed all kinds of athletic exploits, including a First Class in Classical Moderations. He is also a great player of football, who last year helped to represent England in the field, a good shot and an enthusiastic fisherman; while he thinks that he can play golf and billiards in addition. He is an enterprising boy who may always be relied upon to do as well as he is expected to do. He is generally ready for "fun," being full of all the strongest instincts of a young barbarian at play; and, being now at once Captain of the Association Football, President of the Athletic Club and Captain of the Cricket Club at Oxford, it is not too much to say of him that he is the best all-round man that has lately been produced either on the Cam or the Isis.

He is a nice, good-looking young fellow, who can sing a song and can illustrate a note-book with caricatures of his Dons. He is said to be able to speak upon emergency with much readiness, yet he is not without discretion. He is generally liked.

He is sometimes known as "C. B."; but it has lately been suggested that he should be called "Charles III."

1894
Men of the Day No. 584

"Oxford Athletics".

MR JOHN LORAINE BALDWIN

HE is but ten years younger than the nineteenth century; so that his early life is matter of ancient history: nevertheless his name is known throughout Clubland, and wherever the game of cricket is played. He is still full of vitality and good humour; and he has done much that he is proud of. When at Christ Church he was one of a group who worked hard in the cricket field, and acted stage plays by way of relaxation; and it was at a supper that he gave at the Blenheim Hotel to Lord Bessborough (then Mr F. Ponsonby), Mr Spencer Ponsonby (now Sir Spencer Ponsonby-Fane), and Mr R.P. Long, that I Zingari, who have just celebrated their Jubilee, were founded; whose annual Vice-President he was then and is now. He also helped to establish the Four-in-Hand Club; he was chief reviser of the rules of short whist; and he has founded, made rules for, and helped to govern so many other Clubs that he used to be known as the King of Clubs. For more than half a century, indeed, his voice was the voice of a master in Clubland; to which none listened without respect; and he has ever been enequalled as a draughtsman of Club Rules, a great authority on cards, and a general referee in all matters of doubt and detail. He has always been a complete sportsman, a popular fellow, and a big man of much presence. He possesses many treasures and much respect; and for many years he was the compiler of that celebrated scrap-book, "The Chronicles of I Zingari," which is now continued by Sir Spencer Ponsonby-Fane. He is a great friend of the Duke of Beaufort, he lives at St Ann's, hard by the ruins of Tintern Abbey, and he is commonly known as the Bishop of Tintern.

He is a very fine specimen of the English sportsman of the olden time.

1895
Men of the Day No. 630

"I Zingari"

MR R.A.H. MITCHELL

MR Richard Arthur Henry Mitchell is a very popular Eton Master whose years are uncertain. He took Day's House at the corner of Keat's Lane some thirty years ago, and moved to his present House twelve years later; a year or two after he had married. Though he is not a great scholar yet he is an excellent teacher of boys and quite an admirable House Master. He is a very good golfer who began rather late in life; but he dislikes interruption so much that when on the putting green in the spring larks are not allowed to sing overhead, lest they might put him off his stroke. He used to encourage theatricals, but he always drew the line at classical reproductions in classical costume. He has played much excellent cricket, as every cricketer knows, and he has three sons, all of whom were in the Eleven—the newest of them this year; consequently he prefers dry bobs to wet bobs, and has been known to sing in part-songs.

The one thing that he cannot stand is the boy who breaks windows. Yet all the boys like "Mike."

1896
Men of the Day No. 653

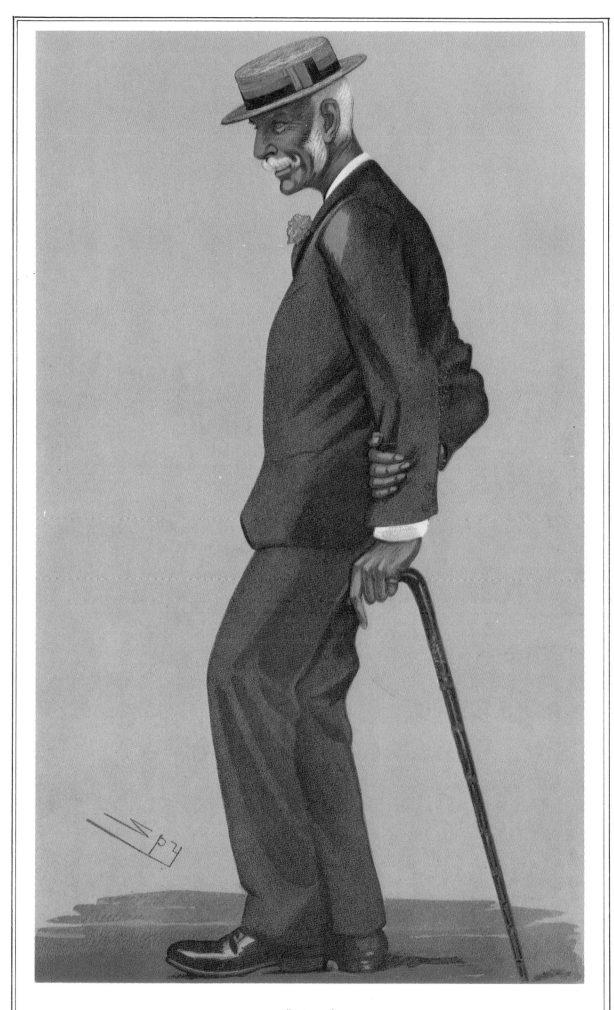

"Mike"

KUMAR SHRI RANJITSINHJI

WITHIN a month of five-and-twenty years ago he was born to Jiwansinhji at Sarodar, in the province of Kathiaward; and was presently adopted by the late Jám of Nawanagar, who was his father's cousin. They began to educate him at Rajkumar College, at Rajkote; but at sixteen he came to England, saw six months of life in London, and went to Trinity, Cambridge: where he learned to play cricket so well that he is now one of the finest bats in the world and a first-rate all-round player. He did not learn much else, but he qualified for Sussex; and last year he made ten centuries and beat Grace's record aggregate.

He is no great scholar, but he is an agreeable lad who dabbles a little in history. He has kept terms at the Bar, and he still keeps his rooms at Cambridge. He mostly lives at Brighton; though he thinks that Lord's is the best cricket ground he knows. His famous leg-glance shows that he has a quick eye; and he can therefore play racquets, and would be very good at billiards if he played less to the gallery. He is also an excellent tennis player, who can hit birds; and, being an all-round sportsman, he fishes and cycles. He is a slim, exceedingly lithe fellow, whose action in the field sometimes reminds you of a panther; and a genial and very casual person, who generally forgets an uncricketing engagement. He does not smoke nor drink, and though he can give extremely cheery parties he professes to keep himself always "fit"; yet is he very popular with men and ladies, and has not done so well this year as he did last. He is very good English company and he speaks unaccented English. When he is travelling he asks at every station what is the sport of the place; he is exceedingly generous, he is always at home, he has a quaint way of telling a good story, he is full of unassuming pluck, and he may be known a mile off by the elasticity of his walk. He has a violent temper, which he generally controls with marked ability; and the people idolise him.

He was first known at Cambridge as "Smith"; but now everyone knows him as "Ranji." He never bets.

1897
Princes No. 19

"Ranji"

CAPTAIN EDWARD WYNYARD

———

HE is a young cricketer who began life on the 1st April seven-and-thirty-years ago; and having learned to play the game at Charterhouse he is now Captain of the Hampshire Cricket Club and a Captain of the Welsh Regiment. He is also Instructor in Fortification at the Royal Military College and he is a good soldier who has smelled powder in Burma, has been mentioned in despatches, and has won a medal and clasp and has the D.S.O.

In the other field he is a good all-round man whose great year was 1894, when his batting brought Hampshire into the list of First-Class Counties, and earned for him a pair of silver candlesticks. His best scoring,—which included three successive centuries,—a then un-paralleled achievement in County matches,—was one of the incidents of that cricket season. Two years ago he did still better, making his top score of 268 against Yorkshire, and ending with an average in all matches,—including Gentlemen v. Players and the final Australian Test Match,—of within a decimal of half a century; and though he has not always batted so well, he is a capital fielder and a useful change bowler, and a reliable wicket-keeper. Apart from cricket, he is an all-round sportsman who has an International football cap for England (Association) and can cut very beautiful figures on the ice. He can hit straight in more ways than one; and he might have gone to Australia with Mr Stoddart. But he did not.

He can speak his mind; and he is supposed to think less of K.S. Ranjitsinhji than some of the public do.

1898
Men of the Day No. 723

"Hampshire."

HH THE MAHARAJA OF PATIALA, GCSI

ALTHOUGH Farzand-i-Khás Daulat-i-Inglishia Mansoor-i-Zaman Amir-ul-Umara Maharaja Dhiraj Rajeshwer Sri Maharaja-i-Rajgan (Sir Rajinder Singh Mahinder Bahadur) became the son of Sir Mahinder Singh, Maharaja of Patiala, only eight-and-twenty years ago, he is now one of the Ruling Chiefs of India and the premier Prince of the Punjaub. He is also the descendant of an ancestor who stood by the English in the Mutiny at a time when his support was worth having; and the head of the Sikhs, a great Chieftain amongst Chiefs, and the leader of a fighting race. As becomes his ancestry, he is himself a keen fighter in the field, and in the polo field; and as a pigsticker he is in the very first flight. A fearless horseman, he is also a good cricketer, who keeps a polo team, a cricket team, and an enormous stable of racehorses—hacks, hunters, and pigstickers—his teams and his horses all giving good accounts of themselves on every occasion: as his *Cherry* did last week, winning the Viceroy's Cup. He is indeed the chief supporter of the Turf in Upper India; and in the late frontier war he went out with his transport and bore himself so well that he was rewarded with the Grand Cross of the Star of India. He is a generous friend, and though he was "privately educated" he is full of quality. He invented the Patiala riding trousers, which are English, and the elastic strap to his turban, which is Sikh. He loves the English in general, and Lord William Beresford in particular; and he has just sent an Arab charger to Lord Roberts.

1900
Princes No. 21

"Patiala"

MR GILBERT LAIRD JESSOP

HE is quite a young fellow lately down from Cambridge—after being a schoolmaster: which is unusual. Yet is he a public character of the biggest sort, for he is, perhaps, the great "draw" of this Cricket Season. As Captain of the Cambridge Eleven he did well; as a County Captain the eyes of the world are upon him—and that, happily, without enlarging his head. For he is a nice boy who knows his place: which is at the wicket. From the moment he gets there he is always hitting, and during the present season his style is better than ever. He is probably the busiest and most active hitter we have had; certainly he is the biggest amateur cricketer of this Century, as many a fast bowler who has seen him jump out and hit him will say; for his quickness of eye and body has made him a terror to them all. He can also bowl fast, though he does less this way than he did before his illness last winter; while as a field he covers more ground than most people think, gathers the ball well, and returns it with a celerity that has amazed many a good batsman. It has indeed been said of him that he saves almost as many runs as he makes. He has captained Gloucestershire for two seasons, and Gloucester idolises him; he plays hockey well and Rugby football with much dash; he will go to Australia with Mr MacLaren in the autumn, and he devotes his leisure to business in the Stock Exchange, where he is almost as popular as he is on the cricket pitch.

The public knows him as the "Croucher"; to his friends he is "Jessopos."

1901
Men of the Day No. 816

"the Croucher"

MR DIGBY LODER ARMROID JEPHSON

HE is one-and-thirty, but he succeeded Mr Key as Captain of the Surrey Eleven in the beginning of the century. Born in Surrey, he played good cricket at Peterhouse; and, with less success, football. For three years he played for Cambridge before he was asked to help in the representation of his County; and he has always supported the Wanderers with his bat. He is a thorough cricketer, who is thought to prefer bowling to batting, though his modesty prevents him from putting himself on so often as he ought. Against the Players at Lord's he once took six wickets for twenty-one runs; and at the Oval he once scored 213 runs off Derbyshire: when he and Abel put on 364 for the first wicket. He is a most dependable person, who scores best on a slow wicket, though he can generally make runs when they are most wanted. He is a nice-looking boy, who has contributed entertainingly to cricket literature. He has also confessed to missing a player through sleeping at extra slip; yet there is no risk of the depreciation of Surrey cricket while he is the Surrey Captain.

They call him the "Lobster," but he has his eccentricities. For he likes music and golf; and he has written a Fairy Tale.

1902
Men of the Day No. 841

"The Lobster"

ROBERT ABEL

"BOBBIE," or "The Guv'nor," as he is very generally called, was born three-and-forty years ago; but he did not play for Surrey until he was twenty-two. That year his batting average for the County was 3; but since then he has made so many records that that one is eclipsed. In 1897 he and Brockwell thrice put on a couple of centuries for one wicket; seven years earlier he scored ten separate centuries, and, for the sixth successive year, scored over 2000 runs; playing against the Gentlemen he has not only made the highest individual score—247—but also the four highest innings in that match at the Oval; and last year he scored 3309 runs in First-Class matches. Yet he was chosen for his bowling. His defence is very strong, his patience is inexhaustible, and he has mastered the medium-paced ball; while he is such a bad bowler that he often gets wickets. He improves with age; for he is a self-made player whose natural qualifications are few; but he believed in himself, and pluck and perseverance have brought him to high estate. He is not much bigger than his bat; but he generally manages to get well over the ball.

1902
Men of the Day No. 842

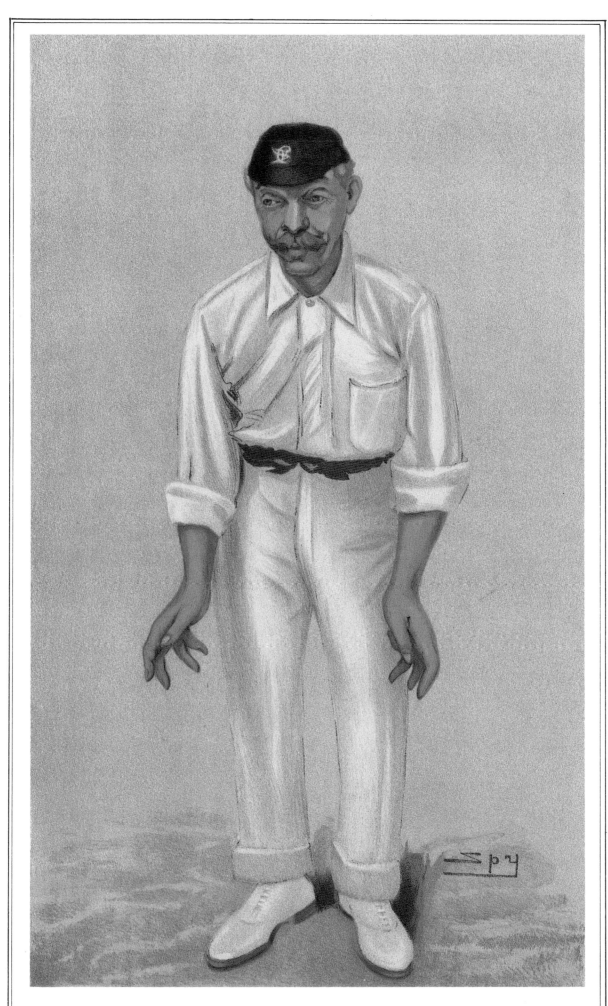

"Bobby"

THE HON. FRANK STANLEY JACKSON, BA

———————

HE is a nice young fellow of two-and-thirty, who may not be obnoxious even to Rudyard Kipling, since he was patriotic enough to give up cricket to serve his country in South Africa: whence he is returned safe and sound and Captain of the 3rd Royal Lancasters, as well as of the Yorkshire Eleven. He is also a director of W.L. Jackson and Sons, Limited; and the son of that Statesman who is just improved by his King into a Peer. Himself was sent to Harrow, where he played cricket; and thence to Trinity, Cambridge, where he played more cricket until he was made Captain of the Light Blue Eleven. Since then he has pretty constantly played for the Gentlemen and for England. He is good at most games, being an excellent shot, a keen man to hounds, and a devoted fisher; but, of course, it is as a cricketer that he has done most for his country. He was first chosen to play for England against Australia in 1893, and he has played in each home match against them since: being, indeed, so capable a player of the game that most people were grieved (and some aggrieved) when, on W.G. Grace's retirement from big matches, he was not called upon to captain the English Eleven. But he still played the game, despite the commiseration of his friends: for, as they say of him, a "better chap never walked." He is now about to plunge into matrimony, so that the other day a fellow-cricketer asked him if he had congratulated the young lady to whom he was to be sacrificed! Yet is he not at all conceited, for he can tell such a story against himself; and another: as when he overheard one of his brother Officers telling others that they had "at last succeeded in making a good chap of him"! He has a jaunty step, a lordly manner, and exceeding confidence in himself: which is a very necessary quality at cricket. He has indeed shown himself the man for a big match, and he is probably the finest all-round cricketer of the day.

He is said to be full of childish simplicity, and he is quite well known as "Jacker."

1902
Men of the Day No. 848

"A Flannelled Fighter"

LIONEL CHARLES HAMILTON PALAIRET

HE is quite a young fellow, who seems to have played the game since he was born, three-and-thirty years ago at Grange-over-Sands. At Repton he captained the Eleven for two years; at Oxford he did the same. On going down he played for Shrewsbury's England Eleven against the Australians in 1893 and for Mr Thornton's Eleven against those visitors three years later. With H.T. Hewett he hit up a record score of 346 against Yorkshire just eleven years ago, and has done many other great things with the bat. Nevertheless, he once ran three miles for Oxford against Cambridge, and he has played football; while he now helps to direct the Newton Electrical Works of Taunton. He is a beautiful player, and whether batting or fielding he is always so graceful that as a pure stylist he is quite unsurpassed. It is not, in fact, possible to see a more engaging batsman when he is in form; and he specially loves the Yorkshire bowling. He comes of a Huguenot family, he is known to his friends as "Coo" and he generally wears a Harlequin cap.

He is a good shot and a capital billiard player.

1903
Men of the Day No. 887

Repton, Oxford & Somerset

GEORGE HIRST

ALTHOUGH he is only two-and-thirty, it is not too much to say that he is the best all-round cricketer of this English generation. Born at Kirkheaton, near Huddersfield, he is a Yorkshireman to the backbone; and for Yorks he has played cricket since 1889, having scored a thousand runs or more and having taken a hundred wickets in four separate seasons. Though he is not so good a sailor as he is cricketer, he is willing to risk the voyages to Australia whenever he is wanted there; for he is full of grit. If he is not a great linguist, he is at least a complete master of the West Riding dialect, who has played for England no fewer than ten times. He bowls with a noted "swerve", he bats with a daring "pull", he fields with all the virtues, and he will ever be remembered as the hero of the England v. Australia match at the Oval last year. His coming "Benefit" should be a well deserved reward; and he may be summed up as a really fine fellow with the heart of a lion.

He has a good appetite and quite a nice smile.

1903
Men of the Day No. 889

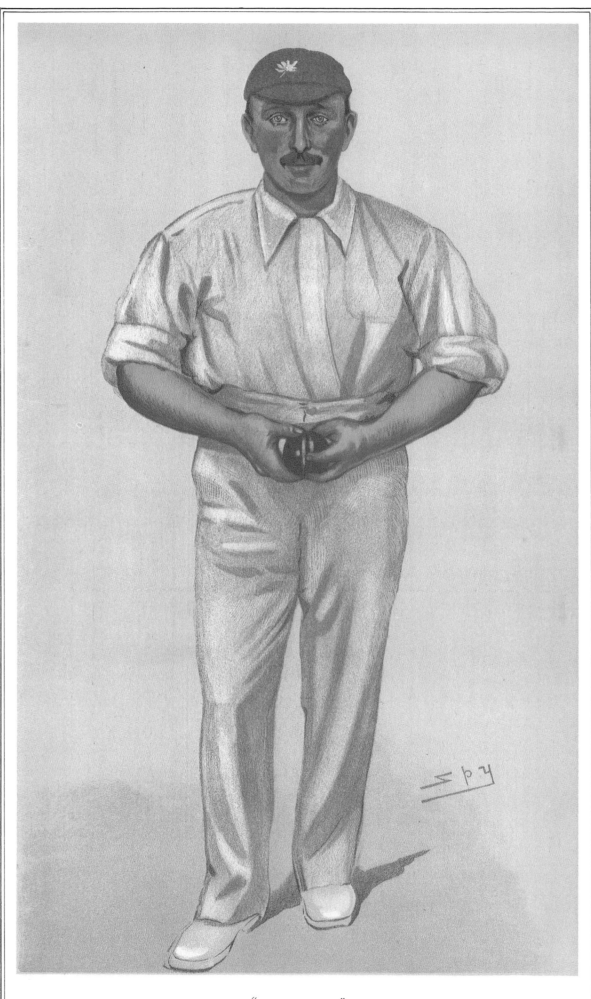

"Yorkshire"

MR PELHAM F. WARNER

JUST thirty years ago he became the youngest son of that West Indian Statesman who steered Trinidad through the trying times that followed the abolition of slavery; of whom Froude said it was worth a voyage round the globe to have met such a man. For his family have been known in the West Indies since the wholesome buccaneering times of Queen Elizabeth; and this particular scion of the house is known as a cricketer all over the world, since he has played in more countries than any other, including the West Indies, Canada, Africa, Australia, New Zealand, and America. His father was privileged to be at Harrow and Eton; but himself has been content with Rugby (where he played in the Eleven for four years), and as an Oriel man, who enjoyed the distinction of being twice run out in the 'Varsity Match. Since then he has been called to the Bar, but he still plays cricket, and on the 25th instant will take a team to Australia which is really good all round and excellent in bowling. He has a cheerful individuality which works wonders, so that they call him an optimist and other bad names; yet he has a very complete knowledge of the game, he knows his "Wisden" by heart, and he studies most carefully his position at the wicket. His great stroke is the on drive; but he wields his pen as skilfully as he does his bat. He is also a good speaker and a good man at a pinch who never loses heart; so that the credit of English cricket is safe in his hands. He generally wears a Harlequin cap, and he is supposed to have been seen uncovered only once, when the Tommies of Barbados violently hoisted him for making the first century scored in the island. He is also very proud of a ring which Lord Hawke gave him for pulling a match out of the fire at Johannesburg four years ago.

He likes criticism, he can play a losing game very well, he is one of the keenest cricketers living, he can keep friends with his men, and he owes his wigmaker a bill.

1903
Men of the Day No. 891

"Plum"

THE EARL OF DARNLEY

HE is descended from one John Bligh of London and Rathmore, in Ireland, who was agent of the Adventurers for the Forfeited Estates in 1641, acquired lands in Meath and became, among other things, a Commissioner for auditing arrears of Customs and Excise, which was probably a sound berth in those good old days. That gentleman was also a Member of Parliament, whose grandson was made the first Earl of Darnley. Himself the eighth Earl, was born just five-and-forty years ago; and as Ivo Bligh, or more familiarly as "Nellie," he was well known wherever cricket is played. For he played the game for Eton (where he now has two boys) for two years; after which he went to Cambridge and played for his University for four years, once as captain. That enabled him to captain the English Eleven in Australia in 1882–3; and led to his marriage with an Australian lady. But apart from cricket—especially Kentish cricket—he is an all-round sportsman as well as a man of manners. At school he won the Racquets for Eton against the other Public Schools; and, as a Light Blue, he beat Oxford at the same game three years running, besides winning two inter-'Varsity contests at tennis. He has since been President of the M.C.C.; but he has now descended to golf. Nevertheless, he is a good shot who is fond of shooting. Once he was on the Stock Exchange, and for several years he was connected with a big firm of port wine shippers; but he is now a Deputy-Lieutenant and a Justice of the Peace for Kent, who owns nine thousand acres of Dickens-land and nearly twice as much in Meath. In Kent also he has a beautiful Elizabethan place known as Cobham Hall, which was built by that Lord Cobham who was father-in-law to the Cecil who built Hatfield. The place came to the Blighs through the heiress of the Dukes of Lennox in the beginning of the eighteenth century; and it is noted for its deer park, its rhododendrons, its woods, and its collection of pictures.

With all his virtues he is an unassuming, upright, very popular fellow with a very gentle voice.

1904
Statesmen No. 766

"Ivo"

VISCOUNT COBHAM

A FREE hitter, a destructive bowler, and an effective wicket-keeper—these were the cricket virtues of Viscount Cobham, who one-and-fifty years ago was born into the world to adorn one of the most illustrious families of Britain.

Four and a half centuries have passed since Thomas Westcote's feats in the field of war attracted the notice of Henry IV and Henry V, and won the heart of Elizabeth, only daughter of Thomas Lyttelton, of South Lyttelton, Worcestershire, whose name he then assumed. Since that happy bridal Lytteltons have lived in Worcestershire, and followed in the footsteps of their ancestor as men of brains, prowess, and muscle. Lord Cobham played for Cambridge against Oxford for four years, and bowled and batted for the Gentlemen of England against the Players for five summers. His father played for Cambridge in 1838, and six of his brothers were in the Eton Eleven of 1872.

"Save me from my relations" can never have been said by the head of the Lytteltons, the present Lord Cobham. He succeeded his father as fifth Baron Lyttelton in 1876, and inherited the Viscounty and Barony of Cobham on the death of the Duke of Buckingham in 1889. Mr Gladstone, Prime Minister of England, was his uncle; Mr Alfred Lyttelton, Secretary of State for the Colonies, is his brother. Another brother was the Bishop of Southampton, and the Bishop of Rochester is his brother-in-law. Sir Neville, yet another brother, is on the Army Council, and the Rev. Edward is Headmaster of Haileybury. Lady Frederick Cavendish and Mrs Talbot, wife of the distinguished M.P. for Oxford University, are sisters. A greater galaxy of talent never issued from beneath an English roof-tree.

Poets are always doing the unexpected thing. So it was that Thomson wrote the "Castle of Indolence" on a seat in Hagley Park, the home of the busiest family in England. Lord Cobham is a Railway Commissioner, a Fellow of Eton College, and a Trustee of the National Portrait Gallery. He stands 6ft. 2in., understands art, believes in exercise, and is the father of four sons and three daughters.

1904
Statesmen No. 767

"Cricket, Railways & Agriculture"

MR B.J.T. BOSANQUET

M R B.J.T. Bosanquet is the best-worst bowler of the present day. Like the heroine of the nursery rhyme, when he is good he is very, very good, and when he is bad he is *horrid*. This fact he will explain to you by several theories of his own construction.

"Bos," as most continents now know him, was publicly introduced to the cricket world by his century in the Eton v. Harrow of '96. It was probably the soundest and undoubtedly the ugliest of all the big scores made in those matches. At Oxford he brought blossoms to a budding reputation, and since he came down he has been in the front of First-Class cricket. He is an inveterate backbone of tours. America, Canada, the West Indies, Australia, and New Zealand have seen him run up scores and capture wickets. There is, indeed, no player of the Anglo-Saxon game better known or better liked wherever pitches are rolled or cocoanut-matting spread.

His most notable successes were achieved last winter with Mr Warner's team in Australia. It will not easily be forgotten how he won a critical Test match for his side by taking five wickets for twelve runs on a pitch in excellent condition. There was never a more sensational bit of bowling. During the season of 1904 he scored over a thousand runs, and captured over a hundred wickets—the hall mark of an all-round cricketer.

He was once a fast bowler, but now delivers "googlies" with artful discrimination. His most dangerous ball is one which seems to have a leg break, but which comes the other way. The typical sangfroid of the Etonian never deserts him. He will argue with you on any point or at any distance from that point. It is immaterial whether he convinces you or not. It is sufficient that he knows. Even his family believe him.

He plays bridge with his head, is useful at croquet, is by no means bad at Soccer, and has a straight eye for billiards. His friends make persistent efforts to see more of him in private life, but the short interval between the close of play and the beginning of dances gives them little opportunity. His enemies have yet to be discovered.

1904
Men of the Day No. 930

"an artful bowler"

LORD DALMENY

THE eldest son of Lord Rosebery has a clever brain and a clear eye. He came of age last year, and the festivities suited the august occasion. Also he made several neat little speeches, causing an admiring tenantry to proclaim his progress on the primrose path that leads to the select if not extensive tabernacle wherein the great ones of Imperial Liberalism assemble.

He captained Eton at football—Wall and Field games—won the racquets, and played a hard-hitting 52 against Harrow till he was caught in front of the Pavilion. It was a good athletic record for a boy to leave behind him. Since then he has played cricket for Middlesex and Bucks; also he has been one of Surrey's many captains during the past season.

In racing and politics he has followed in his father's steps. He has recently registered his colours under the Jockey Club and National Hunt Rules. In this year's Coventry Stakes at Ascot his sympathies must have been strangely divided when his father's crack two-year-old *Cicero* met and defeated *Vedas*, the horse of Mr de Wend Fenton, the closest of his racing friends. He left the Grenadier Guards to become a candidate for Midlothian, and has already attempted to expose the iniquities of the Government in the elegant persiflage of his parent.

He is greatly attached to the art of speech production. He is a fair shot, and has ridden boldly to hounds. He has recently acquired a popular reputation as a hunter of big game. Is not the legend of the mad bull which he slew in his father's park a story over which the tenantry grow pale o' nights? It is rumoured that he has no positive distaste for baccarat. He is now studying languages in Geneva.

He is always called "Harry." The Imperial Radicals believe him to be an Admirable Crichton; but it is not quite so bad as that.

1904
Men of the Day No. 931

"In his father's steps"

THOMAS HAYWARD

IT may be presumed that a batsman who by the first week in July 1906, put together two thousand runs, which total includes ten centuries, is in the prime of his cricketing career. Tom Hayward is five and thirty years old, and plays a difficult bowler with the wisdom of maturity. He has ever been a careful man, and even if he does not rival Dr Grace in cricketing longevity, he should be the backbone of the Surrey batting for another ten years.

He is the son of Daniel Hayward of Cambridge, in which town he was born, and the nephew of Thomas Hayward, still remembered by the veterans among us. That he has no son to follow out the laws of heredity and build up a reputation in his father's declining years is a misfortune which there is still time to remedy, for he is unmarried.

After much youthful cricket at Cambridge he answered an advertisement and found himself at the Oval. His debut was not profitous. In the first match in which he played for Surrey he was bowled without scoring; indeed, it was not until he had played a useful innings against the Australians that he was certain of his place. He prospered, and his reputation grew until he became a notability in a team which contained such men as W.W. Read, Abel, Lockwood, K.J. Key, Richardson and Brockwell.

He has been three times to Australia and once to South Africa. He has played thirteen times against the Australians in this country, with an average of thirty-eight. He scored 158 in the second highest total ever made in a county match, 174 in the highest total ever made by an English team abroad and his highest score is 315 not out.

He is an unassuming fellow with a perfect temper. On a good wicket England has never had a sounder batsman; in earlier days he was a dangerous bowler and a most useful man of his hands in the deep. Mr C.B. Fry has christened him "Thoughtful Tom". It is an appropriate nickname.

1906
Men of the Day No. 1022

"Tom."

MR REGINALD HERBERT SPOONER

REGGIE Spooner has ever evinced a partiality for doing his best on the big occasions, so, after making his biggest score of the season, 82 against Cheltenham, in his first year in the Marlborough Eleven, in the two years following he took centuries at Lord's off the Rugby bowlers; his last innings as a Marlborough boy being 198, after a modest 69 in the first innings of the same match. So impressed were the critics at this brilliant hitting against Rugby that his subsequent triumphs in the next few weeks caused them little surprise. Playing for the Second Eleven of Lancashire against Surrey Second he hit up a splendid innings of 158, then, few days later, making his debut for the county team against Middlesex, he played Albert Trott and J.T. Hearne so effectively that his two innings realised 44 and 83. Nor against the Australians themselves was he less successful, scoring 46 and 31 not out and in his first match, in which the totals on either side were small. All this took place in 1899.

His next appearance in the cricketfield was not until 1903. In the interim he represented England against Wales under the Rugby code and the Queen in the South African war, as a subaltern of the Manchester Regiment, on which Mr Haldene proposed to lay his sacrilegious hands. Since he took to First-Class cricket again in earnest, Mr Spooner has forsaken a martial career for the paths of commerce, but in as much as he no longer plays football, it is only during the summer months he figures prominently before the public eye. He generally makes a score of over 200 runs at least once during the season and can be counted on for an aggregate of 1,200 or 1,500 for his county, while the number of runs he saves in the field has never yet been estimated. Though his feet are very big he invariably stops the ball with his hands.

He is a very popular figure wherever he goes. Well known though he is among athletes, had he gone up to either Oxford or Cambridge his fame would have been even greater, for while at Marlborough, besides his cricket and football triumphs, he excelled at racquets, fives and hockey. He is "Reggie" to his friends, and one day will captain England in a Test match.

1906
Men of the Day No. 1023

"Reggie."

J.T. TYLDESLEY

J.T. Tyldesley was born near Manchester on November 22nd, 1873. As a boy he showed a natural attitude as a batsman. He made his first appearance in First-Class cricket at Old Trafford on July 22nd, 1895, when Gloucester were the visiting team. Thirteen was his total on that occasion—a number not usually connected with subsequent good fortune. However he made 33 runs in the second innings and was not out at the close of the match. Three days later he again appeared for the county against Warwickshire and by playing a sound not out innings of 152 secured for himself a place in the team.

Since that date Tyldesley has played regularly for Lancashire, achieving such a remarkable series of successes that he is now generally acknowledged to be the greatest batsman the county has produced. He has made more runs for the county, more runs per season, more scores of 50 and upwards, more centuries, and has taken part in more century partnerships than any other Lancashire player has done; and he has made as many double century scores as have all the other players combined. Such, in brief, is his record. In First-Class cricket the list of his performance is equally remarkable, whether we examine his doings in such matches as the Gentleman and Players or the reports of his tour in South Africa and Australia. Statistics tend to bore the most enthusiastic, but the statement that in eleven years Tyldesley has scored 46 centuries and scored an average of 42 runs in each of the five hundred innings he has completed is self-explanatory.

He is steady as a batsman and steady as a man. He has an English dislike to fuss and notoriety. Often in Australian towns he has made his way through back streets to avoid the publicity of his admirers in the main thoroughfares. He is generally popular not only with the Lancashire crowds, but with his fellow professionals. Perhaps his best cricketing stroke is off-drive, passing just below cover point. He is a teetotaller.

1906
Men of the Day No. 1026

" Forty-six centuries in eleven years. "

THE REV. F.H. GILLINGHAM

THE Rev. Frank Hay Gillingham was born in Japan in 1875. In due time he entered Dulwich College, where he learned his cricket. On leaving school the City for a time engaged his attention, but a higher call made itself heard, and he resolved to devote his life to the Ministry. He entered St John's Hall, Highbury, and Durham University. Up north he got his "palatinate" for Rugby football and for cricket, at which latter game his average for two seasons was 60 and 80.

Appropriately enough he began his clerical career in 1899 at Leyton, the home of Essex cricket. Here he was one of a succession of athletic curates—his immediate predecessor having been captain of the Durham XI, and his successor being a Cambridge cox.

Owing to his work at Leyton and subsequently to his duties as Chaplain to the Forces at Tidworth, Mr Gillingham has only been able to turn out occasionally. The Essex team chaff him that he picks his wickets, but they know that he prefers to play when his aid is most required and that he has often got the county out of a tight corner. He cannot bowl, but the severest critic of Essex fielding—and there are such people about—could say nothing against Mr Gillingham's excellence in that department of the game. A great feature of his batting is that he succeeds on any wicket, and two or three weeks without practice seem to make no difference to his ability to get runs. His favourite strokes are in front of the wicket, and when he gets set his powerful drives delight the spectators.

His object-lessons at Leyton were celebrated throughout the parish. On one historic occasion he illustrated the elevating effect of fervency of spirit by despatching from the pulpit a fire balloon, which ascended to the ceiling, to the delight of the youthful congregation. The vicar did not hear of the daring experiment till after the service. At Leyton he helped to keep his eye in by having a knock with the boys in some of the back streets on his parochial rounds, and one of the old paupers in the West Ham Union, of which Mr Gillingham was a guardian, quite believes that he is the bowler Essex needs since a certain day when he sent down a clinker that took the cricketing parson's wicket in the union garden.

He now lives with the South Wales Borderers on Salisbury Plain. He rides when he can get anything up to his weight. He fancies himself somewhat in his mess kit. He is a fine preacher, but his reputation on the cricket field gives him a better chance of saving souls than would all the eloquence in the world.

1906
Men of the Day No. 1027

" Cricketing Christianity."

MR C.M. WELLS

IT would be hard to find a better example of *mens sana in corpore sano* than Mr C.M. Wells. Born in London on March 21st, 1871, he went in due course to Dulwich, where, disdaining the usual preliminaries, he spent most of his time in the Sixth Form, and devoted some of his energies to the acquisition of every possible school prize; but that he didn't allow his work altogether to hinder his play is shown by the fact that he was in the Cricket XI from '86 to '90.

In October, 1890, Mr Wells went to Trinity College, Cambridge, with a Major Classical Scholarship, and at Cambridge gained many additional laurels, finally winning a First-Class in the Classical Tripos and the reputation of being one of the best scholars Cambridge has turned out in these latter days.

In September, 1893, Mr Wells became an Eton master, and has now a house which is full till 1916.

His intellectual honours have only been surpassed by his athletic triumphs. After gaining his cricket blue as a Freshman, he was a member of three of the strongest Cambridge XIs of modern times, his contemporaries being such great cricketers as S.M.J. Woods, F.S. Jackson, J. Douglas, K.S. Ranjitsinhji, A.J. Hill, D.L.A. Jephson, and E.C. Streatfield. From 1890–3 Mr Wells played for Surrey, but his sympathies lay more with Middlesex, for which county he has played since '95.

An enthusiastic cricketer, he is rather what may be called an opportunist than a stylist. In his own way he has amassed many runs, his greatest achievement, perhaps, being his 244 for Middlesex *versus* Notts, at Trent Bridge, in 1899. But he is more famous as a bowler and as a field at extra-cover-point than as a bat. As a bowler he has a wonderful command of length, and varies the flight of the ball, using his wits at every moment, so that it is not to be wondered at that he has taken, and still continues to take, many wickets in the brief period in which he can find time for first-class cricket. He has never been known to refuse to bowl, or to refrain from begging for "one more over," and when he gets permission he races off with the ball like a school-boy. His flannels are bought by the yard and would keep two ordinary men warm, even during the present wintry weather, and when the fifth catch has been dropped off his bowling his ejaculations are believed to be taken from Aristophanes.

At Rugby football he was, in every sense of the word, immense: his rushes have been compared to those of a bull, and while his clothes held together were equally hard to stop. He was, indeed, one of the very finest of half-backs, comparable even to that ideal player, A.R. Don Wauchope, and after two seasons in the Cambridge XV, he represented England between 1893 and 1897.

His athletic energies were not satisfied by cricket and Rugby; he also plays golf, at which he drives a very long ball, and the Eton Field game, at which he is almost as good as he was at Rugby football.

Mr Wells is, besides, an entomologist: he likes every sort of bug except humbug. It is possible for a friend to get him to give his views on some subjects—and they are usually found to be vigorous, though orthodox; but as a rule he prefers a quiet dinner and a rubber of bridge to follow.

A few years ago he succeeded the late R.A.H. Mitchell as principal adviser of Eton cricket, and in the last four seasons Eton has won three times and drawn once.

Mr C.M. Wells is as kind as he is strong, and as modest as he is clever; but, like most people whose friendship is worth having, he takes some knowing.

1907
Men of the Day No. 1074

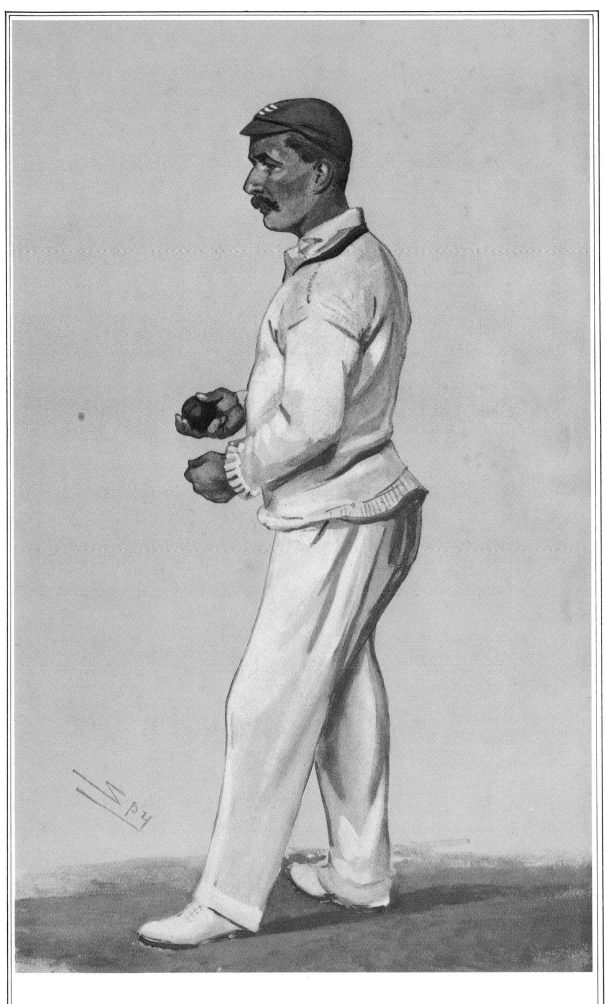

"Father"

MR K.L. HUTCHINGS

MR K.L. HUTCHINGS was born at Southborough, a village near Tunbridge Wells, on December 7th, 1882, and was the youngest of four brothers, all of whom gained their colours at Tonbridge School. K.L. Hutchings was in the XI for five years, and captained the team for the last two, with an average of 47 per innings in 1901 and 62 in 1902.

He was one of the Kent XI, that visited the United States in 1903; but he was hardly known in First-Class cricket till last season, when he was one of the most successful bats in England; he averaged 64·66 for Kent in the County Championship games. Although Hayward was probably the greatest batsman of 1906, it was Mr Hutchings who furnished the sensation of the year. With a style peculiarly his own, he yet showed himself to be one of the finest forcing bats of modern times. He drives with extraordinary vigour—the greatest feature of his game; he can play, too, with facility all round the wicket, while relying for defence on his back-play. Apart from his batting, he is a tireless and excellent out-field, and quite a respectable change bowler.

By scoring two centuries for Kent in their match with Worcestershire, Mr K.L. Hutchings joins the select company who have gained this distinction. C.B. Fry has obtained two separate centuries in one First-Class match on four occasions; W.G. Grace, R.E. Foster, and T. Hayward, each three times; B.J.T. Bosanquet, P.A. Perrin, and J.T. Tyldesley, each twice; while batsmen who have performed the feat on one occasion are G. Brann, A.E. Stoddart, W. Storer, K.S. Ranjitsinhji, A.C. Maclaren (in Australia), Major R.M. Poore, W.L. Foster, G.L. Jessop, H.B. Chinnery, C. McGahey, H. Carpenter, A. Shrewsbury, V. Trumper, E. Arnold, A.O. Jones, J. Seymour, J.H. King, Captain J.G. Greig, L.G. Wright, A.J.L. Hill, G.C.B. Llewellyn, D. Denton, and G.H. Hirst.

Mr K.L. Hutchings is first favourite with the crowd wherever he plays, because he evidently goes in to hit, and scarcely lets a loose ball pass without punishment. All his acquaintances seem to be his friends, and delight in calling him "Hutch." He is a good sportsman, and though he has not achieved all his ambitions, it must be remembered that he is not yet twenty-five, though he has already played for the Gentlemen against the Players.

This year he is so far eighth in batting, with an average of 37·54 for twenty-four innings.

1907
Men of the Day No. 1079

"A Century Maker."

THE HON. ABE BAILEY

IN contempt of damning forecasts and most lamentable predictions South Africa is getting on fairly well since it has been allowed to manage its own affairs. It looks as if Boer and Briton would settle down in peace together without more than the usual difficulties. Of course, South Africa is not so interesting as it used to be. The two great protagonists have been taken away, President Kruger and Cecil Rhodes, and the men who have taken their places are either of smaller stature, or, perhaps it would be truer to say, have less of the limelight of public interest thrown upon them, and are therefore seen less distinctly.

President Kruger's place, however, is ably filled by General Botha and by Mr Smuts. But though less ignorant and more kindly, no one would compare General Botha in elemental power with President Kruger, nor does it seem as if it would be easy to fill Mr Rhodes's place. The man on whom the greater part of the mantle has fallen is assuredly Mr Abe Bailey.

First of all, Mr Abe Bailey has the inestimable advantage of being born and bred in South Africa. He was born of English and Scotch parents at Cradock, in Cape Colony, in 1865, and from childhood he spoke the Taal as easily as he spoke English. He was educated at Clewer House, Windsor, but had too much of the spirit of adventure in him to make much of a hand at book-learning.

In '82 he started as a merchant in Queenstown, speculating in wool. He is one of the few men in the world who made a fortune and lost it before he was twenty-one. In '86 he was in the gold rush to Barberton, but in March '87 returned to Johannesburg and started business for himself as a broker. He was not a prospector, but a man made for the great centres, who fights in the open arena of the Stock Exchange with the ablest for fortune. A rare mixture of cool insight, daring, and resolution gave him victory almost from the start. In the first boom of '89 he speculated boldly and laid the foundation of his great fortune.

After that he went through all the ups and downs of Johannesburg successfully. He is a born gambler; but it is perhaps the Scotch strain in him that gives him the dash of prudence which enables him to keep the money he wins.

It was in '87 that he first met Rhodes in Johannesburg, and their acquaintance soon developed into a close and intimate friendship. He shared the plans of Rhodes; lived with him in closest intimacy for months at a time. And it was not everyone that Rhodes thus took to his heart. There was a certain well-known Jew millionaire whom Rhodes would never allow within his house. He used to wait on the stoep for his audiences, and be dismissed without even a hand-clasp.

Mr Abe Bailey was one of the first to join the Reform Committee in Johannesburg, and in due course he went to prison in Pretoria because of his pro-British sympathies. When the war broke out his side was already chosen. He fought through the war and has two medals with six clasps. He raised Gorringe's column at his own expense and picked the horse and equipment for the C.I.V., whom he considers "a really good lot of men".

He declares that the result of the war is good, that it taught the Boer respect for the Briton, as it certainly taught the Briton respect for the Boer.

Mr Abe Bailey is filled with ideas for the unification of South Africa, and regards Rhodesia as the key-stone of the Arch. "Rhodesia," he says, "is standing out now because Cape Colony and the Transvaal both regard it lightly, on account of its comparatively sparse population. The Rhodesians on the other hand are filled with the idea that they must ultimately become the great state in South Africa, because they have the largest country, and so they are holding out for good terms." Mr Abe Bailey is on the side of Rhodesia and Rhodesia's ambitions.

After Rhodes's death Mr Abe Bailey was selected to succeed him in the Cape Parliament as Member for Barkley West; a few years later he stood in the new Transvaal Parliament for Krugersdorp, and won it by a large majority, though three weeks before the election the betting was ten to one against him. There is a good deal of Rhodes, and something of Kruger too, in Mr Abe Bailey. He may yet combine the best in both influences. He is already a power in South Africa. He owns the *Rand Daily Mail* and he also owns the *Sunday Times* at Johannesburg, which, though a weekly, has the largest circulation in South Africa.

He is an excellent sportsman and athlete, and has played for South Africa at polo and cricket. A man's character is to be found in his hatreds and loves, and Mr Abe Bailey's hatred is against all footling incompetence, while his love is for South Africa and perhaps especially for the wastes of the Karroo. He has a farm on the Karroo, a farm of 200,000 acres, on which he has sixty thousand sheep, five or six thousand head of cattle, besides goats and ostriches innumerable. "The sun-baked Karroo," he says, "is the place to grow healthy and strong; one day when irrigated it will be the garden of South Africa."

1908
Men of the Day No. 1134

94

"Rhodes the Second."

COLIN BLYTHE

THESE biographical notices call for varied treatment. Occasionally egotism must have its way, for unrestrained flattery is often the deadliest sarcasm. Sometimes, too, detail is needed, where the subject is a mere statesman, or one who has made a mark in such trifling things as literature and art. Then—England being as she is—it is necessary to catalogue the great man's achievements, his history, and his freaks.

But Colin Blythe is a cricketer, and—England being as she is—his record needs no recounting. Every schoolboy knows something of Blythe, and treasures it up with the diligent care all too soon to be transferred to politics or petticoats. Every youngster worth his salt can tell you that Blythe was an engineer at Woolwich Arsenal, can tell of his South African and Australian trips, of his slow left-hand teasers, of his spasmodic unreliability as a batsman, and his present position as third in the list of bowling averages. He has already 124 wickets to his credit, and has performed the hat-trick twice.

To these elements of fame he adds a pretty taste for the violin, which he plays in the orchestra conducted by H.C. Steward, another Kent cricketer.

What remains to be said?

1910
Men of the Day No. 1240

"Charlie."

J.B. HOBBS

"HOBBS, J.B.," born in Cambridgeshire on December 16th, 1882, is about the best batsman in the world at present.

All sorts of records in Test cricket are his. He made a thousand runs in this cricket in fewer innings than any other player has ever been able to do.

He has made three successive centuries and aggregated some five hundred runs in consecutive knocks in Test cricket.

In short, he is quite a tested centurion.

What he has done for Surrey would fill a page with figures—all worth printing—but not here.

Hobbs can field second to none at cover-point—in fact, is pretty well in a class by himself in that position.

He specialises in the fine art of shieing at the wicket, and knows more about the way to hit the sticks than most fieldsmen.

He can bowl more than a little, and has been known to swerve a new ball with dire effect; is by no means a bad bowler with an old one either, for that matter.

A pupil of Tom Hayward, he can shift his feet far more quickly than his master. Tom is very proud of his pupil; Jack very ditto of his master—and is always the first to make due acknowledgments.

Personally, Hobbs is one of the very best, one of the very few whom popularity has not spoilt in the least.

He has a happy knack of rising to the biggest occasions—such as first wicket bat for England.

Is a keen collector of "ashes."

1912
Men of the Day No. 2283

"A Tested Centurion."

MR EDWARD WENTWORTH DILLON

KENT'S yearly bid for the County Championship dates from Mr Dillon's acceptance of the captaincy in 1909. In that year and in 1910 Kent were champions. In 1911 they were second in the list, and in 1912, third. This year they are champions once again.

Mr Dillon began playing cricket for Kent in 1900, when he was still at Rugby. He was in the Oxford Elevens of 1901 and 1902. His university career, like that of many other great men, was abbreviated.

He has a way of making a pair of spectacles and has accomplished this feat twice this season. But he is still fonder of making a ''duck'' in the first innings and a century in the second. This is almost a hobby with him.

His bowling average this year is remarkable and, if he was not too good a sportsman to care about averages, the topic might be irksome. It will suffice to say that he does not head the list. Mr Dillon is captain of the most popular sporting county. I wish him luck.

1913
Men of the Day No. 2339

"The Champion County"

CARLO PELLEGRINI

CARLO PELLEGRINI was born at Capua, near Naples, in March, 1839. His father was a land-owner in that place; his mother was a descendant of the Medici family. The strongly individual personality of Carlo ripened early; while still a youth he led the fashion in Naples; he was flattered and courted, and in return for the blandishments of Neapolitan Society he caricatured it good-humouredly in thumbnail sketches. He fought with Garibaldi at the Volturno and at Capua. In November, 1864, he came to London; tasted a little hardship, and was none the worse for it. London Society becoming aware of him, took him to its arms, as Society in Naples had done; but until 1869 it had not occurred to him that, wanting fortune, one must work seriously to live agreeably. He had, however, a fortune in his pencil; and he discovered it, happily for himself and for *Vanity Fair*, when he joined the staff of this journal, in January, 1869, and commenced, with a portrait of Lord Beaconsfield, that wonderful series of cartoons with which his name and fame will be enduringly associated.

Pens that may do so more becomingly than this one, have written that "Ape" during his lifetime had scarcely an equal as a satirical draughtsman, and no superior. His manner originated with him, and in his art as in all else he preserved his individuality to the end. *Vanity Fair* had the great benefit of his services from 1869 until death took the pencil from his fingers in January last; and these were the only pages in which the signature of "Ape"—long since known to Europe and the world—was ever printed. Rejoicing in, and proud of his work, he kept it free from malice; and in this connection it is no mean compliment to his memory to say that not a few of the "Statesmen" and "Men of the Day" whom he caricatured in this journal were, and remained, amongst the staunchest of his friends and the warmest of his admirers.

Man of the world, Bohemian, and a pet of Society, he kept to the last a certain boyish fresh-ness and singular tenderness of heart which, with his vigorous spirits, his gay, fantastic humour, his skill as a raconteur, his odd speech, and his Southern charm of manner, won and main-tained for him friends in every quarter of the town. He had at one time an ambition to excel in oils, and earlier and more careful training in that branch would have enabled him to do so; but his genius and (though he did not always think so) his affections lay in that field of art in which he was so great. Amongst his lesser achievements, he gave his name to a cigarette, snubbed a Duke, and discovered a restaurant. It has been said of him that the statesmen whom he drew will be better known to posterity by his drawings than by their own speeches. His work was absolutely sincere. The pencil of "Ape" never traduced a foe, and never flattered a friend. He hated but one creature under Heaven—the toady.

He died on January 22nd; and we, and others, who once laughed with him, have not yet lacked time to mourn him.

1889
Men of the Day No. 422

"Ape"

MR LESLIE WARD

EIGHTEEN years ago a painter named John Everett Millais introduced to *Vanity Fair* a cartoon of a Man of Science, in the excellence of which, when he came across it in the portfolio of a young man, he had been so greatly delighted that he even supposed it might be good enough to take the fancy of the Pilgrim Leader who was so hard to please. Sir John was himself in the way of being an artist, and he was right; so that through his means an eminent Professor came to be immortalised in *Vanity Fair*. This was the first of Leslie Ward's caricatures, who has since been responsible for something like five hundred portraits in this journal; until now, for the first time, he has refused to provide a drawing in that one for which this week had been set apart. And the name of "Spy" has become as well known as *Vanity Fair* can make it.

Leslie Ward, who was thirty-nine years old on Thursday last, is the eldest son of Edward Matthew Ward, R.A.—himself a clever caricaturist and mimic amongst those who knew him—who married Miss Henrietta Ward, a lady of quite distinct family, whose pictures have been since seen upon the line at the Royal Academy for thirty years past; who was daughter of George Raphael Ward, famous for miniatures and mezzotints, who was son of James Ward, R.A. And being also mixed up in blood with some half-dozen other Royal Academicians, he clearly ought to be full of artistic virtue. Of this he gave early evidence by his caricatures of schoolfellows at Eton—where he learned some Latin and Greek, to which he added under Professor Attewell at Barnes; yet, having given much promise of a lively kind, he was destined by his family to sit on a high stool and to debase his art to the work of architectural draughtsmanship. So he was sent to Mr Sidney Smirke, R.A., who shaped the architectural ends of the Carlton and of Burlington House and of other aristocratic buildings; and for three weary years he tried to imbibe Mr Smirke's ideas without success. So they tried again, and sent him to Sir Edward Barry, R.A., another designer of palaces; but Sir Edward saw the young man's bent, and with the aid of Mr Frith persuaded his father to make an artist of him; so that at last he became a student of the Royal Academy. Then he felt more at his ease; although it is on record that, having seen *Vanity Fair*, he vowed that he could not die happy until he had succeeded in adding his own wares to the merchandise offered by the other Pilgrims.

Leslie Ward has done much good work. At sixteen he had a bust in the Academy, where he has since exhibited as painter in oil and water-colour, and as artist in black and white. He drew portraits of Disraeli, Bulwer Lytton, Mr Gladstone, Sir John Millais, Miss Thompson (now Lady Butler), Sir Frederick Leighton, and of many others, in the *Graphic*; which newspaper alone besides *Vanity Fair* has had any chance of publishing his work. He has painted full-length and life-sized portraits in oil of many notable men and women, among them the only one ever painted of the late Duke of Portland, which he did for the late Lady Ossington, who left it to the present Duke. For *Vanity Fair* he has drawn Kings, Princes, Potentates, Peers, Statesmen, Judges, Soldiers, Sailors, Artists, Authors, Actors, and a Showman, with complete impartiality; so that each drawing has satisfied everyone, except, perhaps, upon occasion, the person drawn. He has also drawn big groups of figures, such as "Eton Football at the Wall," which filled two pages of the *Graphic*. Competent critics have said that he has done the best work that has been seen in *Vanity Fair*; which is high, but not too high, praise of his artistic excellence; and the name "Spy" is not seen in other publications only because Mr Ward has, by legal artifice, devoted himself to the exclusive service of *Vanity Fair*.

He is a very popular young man, with all those easy-going ways of artistic bachelorhood, which make him welcome in the Clubs. He is very conscientious, and nervous with the nervousness of true art; and even his most atrocious caricatures have not made him an enemy. For there is no spite in his work, but only truth. He is a keen sportsman whose quarry is man; and he could tell stories of stalking which would make the most hardened deer-stalker pale with envy. The methods which he has employed, the ruses which he has adopted, the characters which he has assumed, the deceptions which he has practised, the plots which he has hatched, or which he has had hatched for him, would fill a volume; for there are but few men who are so unartificial as to voluntarily offer their portraits for *Vanity Fair*. Most of them must be studied unawares, in order that their counterfeit presentments may be true presentments of them as they really are, and not the graceful presentments which are compassed by sitters in a studio where Nature is consciously or unconsciously superseded by the airs and affectations of Art. Yet, with all his success, he is a very modest man, quite without guile. When in his old age he comes to write his "Reminiscences," that volume will have a big sale.

He makes a great deal of money; but he has a great deal to do with it.

1889
Men of the Day No. 449

"Spy"

APPENDIX I
Artists and their Pseudonyms

Pseudonym	Artist	Date of Work
Ape	Carlo Pellegrini	1839–89
Spy	Sir Leslie Ward	1851–1922
ALS	Identity unknown Contributed only one cartoon	1910
Owl	Identity unknown One cartoon	1913
STUFF	Possibly H.C. Sepping Also possibly H.C. Sepping Wright	1891–1900
WH	Identity unknown	1910–12
PAL	J. de Paleologu One cartoon	1889–90
Bint	Identity unknown One cartoon only	1893
	Melchiorre Delfico	1872–3
Ao	Roland L'Estrange (Ao for Armadillo)	1903–4 and 1907
Lib	Liberio Prosperi	1886–94 and 1902–3
Hay	Identity unknown Contributor	1886, 1888–99
	François Verheyden	1883
CG or FCG	Sir Francis Carruthers Gould	1879, 1890 and 1897–9
MR	Identity unknown Two cartoons	1900–1
Bede	Two cartoons	1905–6
Elf	Contributor	1908–10

APPENDIX II
John Arlott's list of all the cricketers caricatured in
Vanity Fair published in *The Cricketer*, August 22, 1953

Brackets round the date of a cartoon indicate that the date is not given on the
drawing but John Arlott has been able to supply it from the text.

	Name	County or Club	Caption to Cartoon	Date or Number of Cartoon	Artist's Signature
1	W.G. Grace	Gloucestershire	*Cricket*	9.6.1877	Spy
2	F.R. Spofforth	Australia	*The Demon Bowler*	13.7.1878	Spy
3	Lord Harris	Kent	*Kent*	16.7.1881	Spy
4	G.J. Bonnor	Australia	*Australian Cricket*	13.9.1884	Ape
5	Hon. A. Lyttelton	Middlesex	*English Cricket*	20.9.1884	Ape
6	W.W. Read	Surrey	*W.W.*	28.7.1888	Lib
7	H. Philipson	Oxford University and Middlesex	*Oxford Cricket*	29.6.1889	Spy
8	A.N. Hornby	Lancashire	*Monkey*	15.8.1891	Stuff
9	A.E. Stoddart	Middlesex	*A big hitter*	9.7.1892	Stuff
10	S.M.J. Woods	Somerset	*Sammy*	6.8.1892	Stuff
11	Lord Hawke	Yorkshire	*Yorkshire Cricket*	24.9.1892	Spy

Name	County or Club	Caption to Cartoon	Date or Number of Cartoon	Artist's Signature
12 C.B. Fry	Sussex and Hampshire	Oxford Athletics	19.4.1894	Spy
13 J.L. Baldwin	Co-founder of I Zingari	I Zingari	5.9.1895	Spy
14 The 6th Earl of Dartmouth	President of MCC	The Earl of Dartmouth	10.10.1895	Stuff
15 Viscount Curzon (6th Earl Howe)	Eton and Leicestershire	South Bucks	4.6.1896	Spy
16 R.A.H. Mitchell	Eton and Leicestershire	Mike	16.7.1896	Spy
17 C.F.C. Clarke	Surrey	The Consol Market	19.11.1896	Spy
18 D.H. McLean	Somerset	Ducker	8.4.1897	Spy
19 K.S. Ranjitsinhji	Sussex	Ranji	26.8.1897	Spy
20 Capt. E.G. Wynyard	Hampshire	Hampshire	25.8.1898	CG
21 Hon. E. Lyttelton	Middlesex and Worcester	Haileybury	9.5.1901	Spy
22 G.L. Jessop	Gloucester	The Croucher	25.7.1901	Spy
23 Hon. N.G. Lyttelton	Eton and Worcester	4th Division	5.9.1901	Spy
24 D.L.A. Jephson	Surrey	The Lobster	22.5.1902	Spy
25 R. Abel	Surrey	Bobby	5.6.1902	Spy
26 Hon. F.S. Jackson	Yorkshire	A Flannelled Fighter	28.8.1902	Spy
27 Rev. H.M. Burge	Bedfordshire and MCC	Winchester	2.7.1903	Spy
28 L.C.H. Palairet	Somerset	Repton, Oxford & Somerset	6.8.1903	Spy
29 G. Hirst	Yorkshire	Yorkshire	20.8.1903	Spy
30 P.F. Warner	Middlesex	Plum	3.9.1903	Spy
31 Lord Darnley (played as Hon. Ivo Bligh)	Kent	Ivo	7.4.1904	Spy
32 Viscount Cobham (played as Hon. C.G. Lyttelton)	Eton, Cambridge University and Worcester	Cricket, Railways & Agriculture	5.5.1904	Spy
33 B.J.T. Bosanquet	Middlesex	An artful bowler	15.9.1904	Spy
34 Lord Dalmeny	Middlesex and Surrey	In his father's steps	22.9.1904	Spy
35 R.H.B. Marsham	Oxford University	Bow Street	(12.10.1905)	Spy
36 E. Lubbock	Eton and Kent	The Master of the Blankney	4.1.1906	Bede
37 T. Hayward	Surrey	Tom	(11.7.1906)	Spy
38 R.H. Spooner	Lancashire	Reggie	(18.7.1906)	Spy
39 J.T. Tyldesley	Lancashire	Forty-six centuries in eleven years	(8.8.1906)	Spy
40 Rev. F.H. Gillingham	Essex	Cricketing Christianity	(15.8.1906)	Spy
41 C.M. Wells	Surrey and Middlesex	Father	(10.7.1907)	Spy
42 K.L. Hutchings	Kent	A Century Maker	(14.8.1907)	Spy
43 Sir A.C. Lucas	Harrow, Surrey and Middlesex	Arthur	(2.6.1909)	Elf
44 C. Blythe	Kent	Charlie	(3.8.1910)	ALS
45 J.B. Hobbs	Surrey	A Tested Centurion	(8.1912) 2283	WH
46 E.W. Dillon	Kent	The Champion County	(8.1913) 2339	Owl
47 Sir A. Bailey	Transvaal	Rhodes the Second	9.9.08(1134)	Spy

J.W. Goldman's additional list published in
The Cricketer, September 5, 1953

Name	County or Club	Caption to Cartoon	Date or Number of Cartoon	Artist's Signature
1 Duke of Beaufort, KG	President, MCC	The Duke of Sport	30.8.1876	Spy
2 6th Earl of Bessborough	Harrow, Cambridge University, MCC and I Zingari	Fred	20.10.1888	Spy
3 Mr Justice Bray	Westminster, Cambridge University and Surrey	A man of Law and Broad Acres	17.10.06	Spy
4 Rev. H.M. Butler	Harrow XI, 1851	Trinity	28.5.1903	Spy
5 Lord Chelmsford	Formerly Thesiger	Isandula	3.9.1881	Spy
6 C.C. Clarke	Surrey and Esher		19.11.1896	Spy
7 1st Earl of Dudley	Oxford University, 1841–2. President, MCC	Property	18.6.1870 544	Ape
8 Lord Geo. Hamilton	Harrow. President, MCC	Georgie	5.4.1879	Spy
9 E. Horsman	Rugby and Cambridge University	The Eccentric Liberal	10.8.1872	
10 Thomas Hughes	Rugby and Oxford University		8.6.1872	
11 2nd Earl of Leicester	President, MCC, 1848	Agriculture	4.8.1883	Spy
12 Rt. Hon. W.H. Long	Harrow. President, MCC, 1906	Wiltshire	16.10.1886	Spy
13 Lord Lyttelton	Eton and Cambridge University	A man of position	1.4.1871	Ape
14 Hon. G.W. Spencer Lyttelton	Eton and Cambridge Univeristy	Marshal of the Ceremonies	4.12.1875	Ape
15 General Fredk Marshall	President, Surrey CCC	Fred	24.12.1896	Spy
*16 HH the Maharaja of Patiala	All-India Team of 1911	Patiala	4.1.1900	MR
17 Rt. Hon. Sir Spencer Ponsonby-Fane	Treasurer, MCC. President, Somerset CCC	Spencer	26.1.1878	Spy
18 1st Earl Loreburn	Cheltenham, Kent and Oxford University	Mr Attorney	10.1.1895	Spy
19 Rev. Dr J.C. Ryle	Eton and Oxford University	Liverpool	26.3.1881	Ape
20 Lord Charles Russell	President, MCC, 1835	This fell sergeant—strict in his arrest	12.4.1873	
21 P.M. Thornton	Harrow and Middlesex		22.3.1900	Spy
22 J.R. Mason	Supplement to *The World*			Spy

*Not a member, but a patron of All-India 1911

Batting						Player	Appearance	Bowling			Hundred Wickets in Season
Innings	Runs	Not Out	Highest Score	100s	Average		First/Last	Runs	Wickets	Average	
1007	33124	73	357*	73	35.46	R. Abel	1881/1904	6314	263	24.00	—
582	4415	133	82*	0	9.83	C. Blythe	1899/1914	42099	2503	16.81	14†
244	4820	17	128	5	21.23	C.J. Bonnor	1880/1891	470	12	39.16	—
382	11696	32	214	21	33.42	B.J.T. Bosanquet	1898/1919	14974	629	23.81	1
164	3551	6	138	2	22.47	Lord Dalmeny	1902/1920	100	3	33.33	—
261	11006	25	143	15	28.29	E.W. Dillon	1900/1923	2426	74	32.78	—
658	30886	43	258	94	50.22	C.B. Fry	1892/1922	4872	166	29.34	—
352	10050	24	201	19	30.64	F.H. Gillingham	1903/1928	12	0	—	—
1478	54210	104	344	124	39.30	W.G. Grace	1865/1908	50952	2809	18.13	8
394	9898	24	176	10	26.75	Lord Harris	1870/1911	1779	75	23.72	—
936	16750	105	166	13	20.15	Lord Hawke	1881/1912	16	0	—	—
1138	43551	96	315*	104	41.79	T.W. Hayward	1893/1914	11042	481	22.95	—
1217	36356	152	341	60	34.13	G.H. Hirst	1891/1929	51366	2742	18.73	15†
1324	61749	106	316*	199	50.69	J.B. Hobbs	1905/1934	2688	108	24.89	—
710	16108	41	188	16	24.08	A.N. Hornby	1867/1899	258	11	23.45	—
311	10054	12	176	22	33.62	K.L. Hutchings	1902/1912	926	24	38.58	—

* not out   † 200 wickets in one season

Date of Appearance in Vanity Fair	Subject	Caption	Vanity Fair Reference	Artist	School
9.6.1877	William Gilbert Grace	Cricket	Men of the Day No. 150	Spy	Bristol Medical School
13.7.1878	Frederick Robert Spofforth	The Demon Bowler	Men of the Day No. 183	Spy	
16.7.1881	Lord Harris	Kent	Statesmen No. 364	Spy	Eton
13.9.1884	George John Bonnor	Australian Cricket	Men of the Day No. 313	Ape	
20.9.1884	Honourable Alfred Lyttelton	English Cricket	Men of the Day No. 314	Ape	Eton
28.7.1888	Walter William Read	W.W.	Men of the Day No. 406	Lib	
29.6.1889	Hylton Philipson	Oxford Cricket	Men of the Day No. 429	Spy	Eton
15.8.1891	Albert Nielson Hornby	Monkey	Men of the Day No. 513	Stuff	Harrow
9.7.1892	Andrew Ernest Stoddart	A big hitter	Men of the Day No. 543	Stuff	Private
6.8.1892	Samuel Moses James Woods	Sammy	Men of the Day No. 544	Stuff	Brighton College
24.9.1892	Lord Hawke	Yorkshire Cricket	Statesmen No. 601	Spy	Eton
19.4.1894	Charles Burgess Fry	Oxford Athletics	Men of the Day No. 584	Spy	Repton
26.8.1897	Kumar Shri Ranjitsinhji	Ranji	Princes No. 19	Spy	
25.8.1898	Capt. Edward George Wynyard	Hampshire	Men of the Day No. 723	CG	Charterhouse
25.7.1901	Gilbert Laird Jessop	The Croucher	Men of the Day No. 816	Spy	Cheltenham Grammar
22.5.1902	Digby Loder Armroid Jephson	The Lobster	Men of the Day No. 841	Spy	Manor House, Clapham
5.6.1902	Robert Abel	Bobby	Men of the Day No. 842	Spy	
28.8.1902	Honourable Frank Stanley Jackson	A Flannelled Fighter	Men of the Day No. 848	Spy	Harrow
6.8.1903	Lionel Charles Hamilton Palairet	Repton, Oxford & Somerset	Men of the Day No. 887	Spy	Repton
20.8.1903	George Hirst	Yorkshire	Men of the Day No. 889	Spy	
3.9.1903	Pelham Francis Warner	Plum	Men of the Day No. 891	Spy	Rugby
15.9.1904	Bernard James Tindall Bosanquet	An artful bowler	Men of the Day No. 930	Spy	Eton
22.9.1904	Lord Dalmeny	In his father's steps	Men of the Day No. 931	Spy	Eton
11.7.1906	Thomas Hayward	Tom	Men of the Day No. 1022	Spy	
18.7.1906	Reginald Herbert Spooner	Reggie	Men of the Day No. 1023	Spy	Marlborough
8.8.1906	John Thomas Tyldesley	Forty-six centuries in eleven years	Men of the Day No. 1026	Spy	
15.8.1906	Rev. Frank Hay Gillingham	Cricketing Christianity	Men of the Day No. 1027	Spy	Dulwich
10.7.1907	Cyril Mowbray Wells	Father	Men of the Day No. 1074	Spy	Dulwich
14.8.1907	Kenneth Lotherington Hutchings	A Century Maker	Men of the Day No. 1079	Spy	Tonbridge
3.8.1910	Colin Blythe	Charlie	Men of the Day No. 1240	ALS	
7.8.1912	John Berry Hobbs	A Tested Centurion or Test Cricket	Men of the Day No. 2283	WH	
3.9.1913	Edward Wentworth Dillon	The Champion County	Men of the Day No. 2339	Owl	Rugby

Batting						Player	Appearance	Bowling			
Innings	Runs	Not Out	Highest Score	100s	Average		First/Last	Runs	Wickets	Average	Hundred Wickets in Season
505	15901	35	160	31	33.83	F.S. Jackson	1890/1907	15791	774	20.40	1
313	7973	53	213	11	30.66	D.L.A. Jephson	1890/1904	7457	297	25.04	—
855	26698	37	286	53	32.63	G.L. Jessop	1894/1914	19904	873	22.80	2
171	4429	12	181	7	27.85	A. Lyttelton	1876/1887	172	4	43.00	—
488	15777	19	292	28	33.63	L.C.H. Palairet	1890/1909	4849	143	33.91	—
139	1951	27	150	2	17.41	H. Philipson	1887/1898	—	—	—	—
500	24692	62	285*	72	56.37	K.S. Ranjitsinhji	1893/1920	4601	133	34.59	—
749	22349	52	338	38	32.06	W.W. Read	1873/1897	3482	108	32.26	—
236	1928	41	56	0	9.88	F.R. Spofforth	1874/1897	12759	853	14.95	2†
393	13681	16	247	31	36.28	R.H. Spooner	1899/1923	581	6	96.83	—
537	16738	16	221	26	32.13	A.E. Stoddart	1885/1900	6570	278	23.63	—
994	37897	62	295*	86	40.66	J.T. Tyldesley	1895/1923	211	3	70.33	—
875	29028	76	244	60	36.33	P.F. Warner	1894/1929	636	15	42.40	—
219	4229	27	244	4	22.03	C.M. Wells	1891/1909	9235	465	19.86	—
690	15345	35	215	19	23.42	S.M.J. Woods	1886/1910	21653	1040	20.82	2
272	8318	20	268	13	33.00	E.G. Wynyard	1878/1912	2130	66	32.27	—

Statistics supplied by the Association of Cricket Statisticians

University and Further Education	County or State	Country	Date of Birth	Date of Death
St Bartholomews and Westminster	Gloucester	England	18.7.1848	23.10.1915
	New South Wales, Victoria and Derbyshire	Australia	9.9.1853	4.6.1926
Oxford	Kent	England	3.2.1851	24.3.1932
	New South Wales and Victoria	Australia	22.2.1855	27.6.1912
Cambridge	Middlesex	England	7.2.1857	7.5.1913
	Surrey	England	23.11.1855	6.1.1907
Oxford	Middlesex	England	8.6.1866	4.12.1935
	Lancashire	England	10.2.1847	17.12.1925
	Middlesex	England	11.3.1863	3.4.1915
Cambridge	Somerset	Australia and England	14.4.1868	30.4.1931
Cambridge	Yorkshire	England	16.8.1860	10.10.1938
Oxford	Surrey, Sussex and Hampshire	England	25.4.1872	7.9.1956
Cambridge	Sussex	England	10.9.1872	2.4.1933
	Hampshire	England	1.4.1861	30.10.1936
Cambridge	Gloucester	England	19.5.1874	11.5.1955
Cambridge	Surrey		23.2.1871	19.1.1926
	Surrey	England	30.11.1857	10.12.1936
Cambridge	Yorkshire	England	21.11.1870	9.3.1947
Oxford	Somerset	England	25.6.1871	11.2.1955
	Yorkshire	England	7.9.1871	10.5.1954
Oxford	Middlesex	England	2.10.1873	30.1.1963
Oxford	Middlesex	England	13.10.1877	12.10.1936
	Middlesex and Surrey		8.1.1882	30.5.1974
	Surrey	England	23.9.1871	19.7.1939
	Lancashire	England	21.10.1880	2.10.1961
	Lancashire	England	22.11.1873	27.11.1930
Durham	Essex		6.9.1875	1.4.1953
Cambridge	Middlesex		21.3.1871	22.8.1963
	Kent	England	7.12.1882	3.9.1916
	Kent	England	30.5.1879	Nov. 1917
	Surrey	England	16.12.1882	21.12.1963
Oxford	Kent		15.2.1881	25.4.1941

APPENDIX IV
Vanity Fair Cricketers: MCC Tours and Presidents

MCC Tours
To Australia

1903–4	1907–8	1911–12	1920–1
P.F. Warner	K.L. Hutchings	P.F. Warner	J.B. Hobbs
B.J.T. Bosanquet	J.B. Hobbs	J.B. Hobbs	
T. Hayward	C. Blythe		
J.T. Tyldesley			
G.H. Hirst			

To South Africa

1905–6	1909–10	1913–14
P.F. Warner	Capt. E.G. Wynyard	J.B. Hobbs
Capt. E.G. Wynyard	J.B. Hobbs	
C. Blythe	C. Blythe	

To New Zealand	To United States	To Egypt
1906–7	1907	1909
Capt. E.G. Wynyard	Capt. E.G. Wynyard	Capt. E.G. Wynyard

Presidents of MCC in Office Before 1868

Year of Office	Date of Cartoon	Name of President	Caption	Vanity Fair Reference	Artist	Remarks
1835	12.4.1873	Lord Charles Russell	*This fell sergeant*	Men of the Day No. 61		
1848	4.8.1883	2nd Earl of Leicester	*Agriculture*	Statesmen No. 429	Spy	
1849	21.12.1893	6th Earl of Darnley	*Cobham Hall*	Statesmen No. 627	Spy	
1859	13.8.1881	9th Earl of Coventry	*Covey*	Statesmen No. 368	Ape	
1860	15.7.1871	Lord Skelmersdale	*A Conservative Whip*	Statesmen No. 88	Ape	
1861	2.7.1870	5th Earl Spencer	*The Messenger of Peace*	Statesmen No. 53	Ape	
1862	3.5.1894	4th Earl of Sefton	*Earl of Sefton*	Statesmen No. 635	Lib	
1863	3.5.1879	5th Baron Suffield	*Charlie*	Statesmen No. 301	Ape	
	17.7.1907		*Suffield*	Statesmen No. 1075	Ao	
1864	18.6.1870	1st Earl of Dudley	*Property*	Statesmen No. 52	Ape	
1865		1st Baron Ebury				
1866		7th Earl of Sandwich				
1867		2nd Earl of Verulam				

Presidents of MCC 1868–1913

Year of Office	Date of Cartoon	Name of President	Caption	Vanity Fair Reference	Artist	Remarks
1868		2nd Baron Methuen				See Note 1
1869	4.4.1874	5th Marquess of Lansdown	*Family*	Statesmen No. 166	Ape	
1870		J.H. Scoursfield				
1871	10.1.1901	5th Earl of Clarendon	*The Lord Chamberlain*	Statesmen No. 731	Ape	
1872	27.10.1883	8th Viscount Downe	*Smartness*	Statesmen No. 436	Spy	
1873		Viscount Chelsea				
1874	5.3.1881	Marquess of Hamilton	*Hamlie*	Statesmen No. 357	Spy	
1875		Sir Charles Legard				
1876	19.10.1878	2nd Lord Londesborough	*A Whip*	Statesmen No. 287	Spy	See Note 2
1877	30.9.1876	8th Duke of Beaufort	*Duke of Sport*	Statesmen No. 233	Spy	
	7.9.1893		*Badminton*	Statesmen No. 618	Spy	

Year of Office	Date of Cartoon	Name of President	Caption	Vanity Fair Reference	Artist	Remarks
1878		2nd Lord Fitzhardinge				
1879		W. Nicholson				
1880	4.9.1875	Sir William Start-Dyke	A Whipper	Statesmen No. 213	Ape	
1881	5.4.1879	Lord George Hamilton	Georgie	Statesmen No. 298	Spy	
1882		2nd Baron Belper				
1883		Robert Grimston				
1884		5th Earl Winterton				See Note 3
1885	28.1.1893	3rd Baron Wenlock	Madras	Statesmen No. 608	Bint	
1887		Hon. Edward Charles Leigh				
1888		6th Duke of Buccleuch				See Note 4
1889	7.3.1874	Sir Henry James	Nervous	Statesmen No. 164	Ape	
1890	30.7.1881	22nd Baron Willoughby de Eresby	A great officer of State	Statesmen No. 366	Spy	as 2nd Lord Aveland
1891		V.E. Walker				
1892		W.E. Denison				See Note 5
1893	10.10.1895	6th Earl of Dartmouth	Earl of Dartmouth	Statesmen No. 658	Stuff	
1894	11.10.1890	7th Earl of Jersey	New South Wales	Statesmen No. 574	Spy	
1895	16.7.1881	4th Baron Harris	Kent	Statesmen No. 364	Spy	
1896		14th Earl of Pembroke				See Note 6
1897		3rd Earl of Lichfield				
1898	20.9.1884	Hon. Alfred Lyttelton	English Cricket	Men of the Day No. 314	Ape	
1899	3.11.1888	Sir Archibald L. Smith	3rd Commissioner	Judges No. 24	Spy	
1900	7.4.1904	Hon. Ivo Bligh	Ivo	Statesmen No. 766	Spy	
1901	4.6.1896	4th Earl Howe	South Bucks	Statesmen No. 672	Spy	See Note 7
1902		A.G. Steel				
1903	26.5.1883	Richard Everard Webster QC	Law & Conscience	Men of the Day No. 286	Verheyden	
1903	1.11.1900	1st Baron Alverstone	Dick	Judges No. 57	Spy	
	15.1.1913		Lord Chief Justice	Men of the Day No. 2307	Verheyden	See Note 8
1904		Marquess of Granby				
1905		C.E. Green				
1906	16.10.1886	Rt Hon. W.H. Long	Wiltshire	Statesmen No. 503	Spy	
1907	10.1.1895	1st Baron Loreburn	Mr Attorney	Statesmen No. 646	Spy	as Sir Robert Thresher Reid, QC, MP
1908		3rd Earl Cawdor				
1909	27.1.1909	10th Earl of Chesterfield	A Dandy	Men of the Day No. 1156	Spy	
1910		2nd Earl of Londesborough				See Note 2
1911	20.12.1890	1st Lord Desborough	Taplow Court	Men of the Day No. 492	Spy	
1912		9th Duke of Devonshire				See Note 9
1913		Earl of Dalkeith				

Notes to Table of MCC Presidents

Note 1 Cartoon dated 17 December, 1891 entitled 'The Home District', subject, Major General Lord Methuen, refers to the 3rd Baron.

Note 2 Lord Londesborough, cartoon dated 19 October, 1878—the biography states, 'is the eldest son of Baron Denison . . . a patron of cricket'. Lord Londesborough became the 1st Earl and his son was President MCC in 1910.

Note 3 The cartoon published in 1908, entitled 'A Sticker', refers to the 6th Earl.

Note 4 Cartoon dated 25 January, 1873, 'The Governing Classes'—The Duke of Buccleuch & Queensbury, refers to 5th Duke.

Note 5 The publication dated 1870 of Mr Speaker Denison, 'The first of the Commoners' does not relate to William Evelyn Denison, President MCC in 1892 but to Rt Hon. John E. Denison, a Liberal politician and Speaker to the Parliaments of 1857, 1859, 1866 and 1868.

Note 6 'The Earl & the Doctor' published in 1888 refers to the 13th Earl of Pembroke and Montgomery.

Note 7 The cartoon published 4 June, 1896, 'South Bucks', refers to George

Richard Penn Curzon, eldest son of the 3rd Earl Howe; Viscount Curzon MP. Later of course to become the 4th Earl.

Note 8 Richard Everard Webster became Lord Alverstone and, as well as being the subject of the three cartoons already listed, he was also the central figure of the double size cartoon published in 1902, 'The Heads of Law', a composite picture of the Law Lords.

Note 9 Two cartoons were published of the Duke of Devonshire, one in 1874, the other in 1902, captioned 'Position' and 'Education and Defence' respectively. Neither refers to the 9th Duke, President in 1912.

Additional note President of MCC in 1858, was Lord Garlies. A cartoon 'Army Re-organisation', 10th Earl of Galloway, Baron Garlies, issued on 1 February, 1873 related to Alan Plantagenet Stewart, then aged thirty-six and therefore not President in 1858.

AUTHOR'S NOTE

Wherever possible, I have acknowledged in the text the source of information used. Notable exceptions to this generality relate to Mr Reginald Bosanquet who kindly lent me a number of scrap-books kept by his father and grandfather and also to the catalogue and introduction, prepared by Eileen Harris, relating to the exhibition of original *Vanity Fair* cartoons at the National Portrait Gallery in 1976, from which I drew much valuable material.

During the course of my research and the assembling of the collection, I have visited many antiquarian booksellers and found unfailing help. Lastly, I should like to pay tribute to the staff of the National Portrait Gallery for their kindness and attention and to Mr Stephen Green, Curator, MCC Library at Lord's, whose help was much appreciated and invaluable in providing details of Presidents of long ago.

The lists in Appendix·II are reproduced by courtesy of *The Cricketer International*.

Print dealers selling Vanity Fair *prints*
Burden Clive A., 93, Lower Sloane St, London SW1 W8DA

Burlington Gallery Ltd, 10, Burlington Gardens, London W1X 1LG

Marlborough Sporting Gallery, 6, Kingsbury Street,
Marlborough, Wilts.

McKenzie J.W., 12, Stoneleigh Park Road, Ewell, Surrey KT19 0QT

*Mount Ephraim Books, 25–7, Mount Ephraim, Tunbridge Wells,
Kent TN4 8AE

*Talbot Court Galleries, 7, Talbot Court, Stow on the Wold,
Gloucester GL54 1BQ

indicates sale of reproduction as well as original prints.
Status clearly indicated.

Usually these dealers are able to offer a very limited selection of cricketers. Also watch for advertisements in cricket magazines, collectors magazines and the antique trade books.